ROUTLEDGE LIBRARY EDITIONS:
POLITICAL PROTEST

Volume 20

RESISTANCE AGAINST TYRANNY

RESISTANCE AGAINST TYRANNY

Edited by
EUGENE HEIMLER

Routledge
Taylor & Francis Group

LONDON AND NEW YORK

First published in 1966 by Routledge & Kegan Paul Limited

This edition first published in 2022
by Routledge
2 Park Square, Milton Park, Abingdon, Oxon OX14 4RN

and by Routledge
605 Third Avenue, New York, NY 10158

Routledge is an imprint of the Taylor & Francis Group, an informa business

© 1966 Eugene Heimler

British Library Cataloguing in Publication Data
A catalogue record for this book is available from the British Library

ISBN: 978-1-03-203038-8 (Set)
ISBN: 978-1-00-319086-8 (Set) (ebk)
ISBN: 978-1-03-203376-1 (Volume 20) (hbk)
ISBN: 978-1-03-203377-8 (Volume 20) (pbk)
ISBN: 978-1-00-318701-1 (Volume 20) (ebk)

DOI: 10.4324/9781003187011

Publisher's Note
The publisher has gone to great lengths to ensure the quality of this reprint but points out that some imperfections in the original copies may be apparent.

Disclaimer
The publisher has made every effort to trace copyright holders and would welcome correspondence from those they have been unable to trace.

RESISTANCE AGAINST TYRANNY

A symposium edited by
Eugene Heimler

ROUTLEDGE AND KEGAN PAUL
LONDON

First published 1966
by Routledge & Kegan Paul Limited
Broadway House, 68-74 Carter Lane
London, E.C.4

Printed in Great Britain
by C. Tinling & Co. Ltd., Liverpool

CONTENTS

THE CONTRIBUTORS

Born in 1889 into a farming family in Co. Antrim, *Ernest Blythe* journeyed to Dublin at the age of 16 and a year later joined the Sinn Fein. As a young man and a Member of the Irish Republic Brotherhood, he was deported to England and was imprisoned there in company with the leaders of the Irish Revolt. On his release he returned to Ireland, and under threat of further deportation and extradition orders, continued to work for Ireland's freedom. A journalist, he was Editor of a prominent Republican newspaper, and was elected to the National Executive of the Sinn Fein, eventually serving further terms of imprisonment. He has held ministerial posts in the Underground Republican Government and was Minister of Local Government in the first post-Treaty Dail and became Minister of Finance. A member of the Board of the Abbey Theatre since 1935, he became Managing Director in 1941.

Gisèle Halimi was born in Tunis in 1927, and after reading Philosophy and Law at the Sorbonne, was called to the Bar in Paris in 1949. She has devoted her professional life to defending victims of tyranny, especially in North Africa, and gained international reputation in the case of Djamila Boupacha, about whom Gisèle Halimi published a book in 1962. During the troubles in Algeria in 1958 Mme. Halimi was arrested and held by the Military Authorities on account of her liberal opinions, for three anxious weeks. Her book on Boupacha provides very disturbing evidence about the Algerian episode, and the excesses which were committed at that time. Gisèle Halimi is married and has three sons.

Born in 1922 in Szombathely (Hungary), *Eugene Heimler* matriculated at the Jewish Gymnasium in Budapest in 1943 and during the War was deported to Auschwitz and Buchenwald and several other camps. He later studied at the Academy of Social Science, Budapest and at the London School of Economics and finally qualified at Manchester University in 1953. The author of several books, including poems, he participated in the symposium *Prison*, edited by George Mikes, and has written several articles on literature and social work. He is the Social Work Organiser and Adviser on Health Education to the London Borough of Hounslow and Adviser to the National Assistance Board on Human Relations Training and Community Care, and also lectures on Human Relations at London University.

Colonel *Wolfgang Müller* was born at Bad Rehburg, near Hanover in 1901, the son of a lung specialist. He entered the Royal Prussian Cadet Corps in 1912 and began his military career in 1919 as an Ensign, and later, as a professional infantry officer, specialized in compiling training manuals. He became a journalist at the end of the War and since 1957 has been Editor-in-Chief of a military periodical. He is married and has five children.

Waclaw Zagorski was born in Kiev, Ukraine, on August 28, 1909. He went to school first in Kiev, then in Warsaw, where he later studied law at Warsaw University. Following in the footsteps of his father, a lawyer, journalist and political columnist, he started, while still studying, working as a journalist on daily papers, and at the same time publishing and editing students' magazines. In the years 1929-36, he was one of the leaders of Polish democratic youth, fighting the influences of Fascist and Nationalistic groups. Called up in 1939 he took part in the fighting against the Germans.

During Hitler's occupation of Poland he hid under various pseudonyms. Founder and leader of the underground Socialist group 'Freedom', he organized and directed secret printing works in Wilno, Kielce and Warsaw. He led Socialist partisan units in Central Poland and worked in co-operation with the Jewish Socialist Organization 'Bund'. During the Warsaw uprising in 1944 he led a battalion of worker volunteers, which fought for 63 days in the streets of Warsaw. The diary of this fighting was published in English in 1957 in the book entitled *70 Days*.

He was wounded twice in the fighting with Germans in July 1943 and September 1944. He received the highest Polish order for bravery and valour 'Virtuti Militari'.

After the surrender of the Warsaw Insurrection he was deported to Germany, freed from a P.O.W. camp by American troops in May 1945 and signed up with the Polish army in the West.

At present he lives in London, and is a member of the Central Committee of the Polish Socialist Party in Exile and of the Council of Polish National Unity.

Dr. *André Ungar* was born in 1929. During the war he was forced into hiding from the Nazis in Budapest, with his sister, brother and parents. He later finished his University studies in England, and is a Graduate of the Rabbinical Academy. As a Rabbi of the Reform Movement he held several posts and has worked at the Bernard Baron Settlements in the East End of London. He was a Rabbi in Port Elizabeth, South Africa, in Canada, and Newark, being presently Rabbi of the Conservative Community of Westwood, New Jersey, U.S.A. A Lecturer, he talks widely about the problem of race relations, and has written several articles and pamphlets, of which the best known is 'Living Judaism'.

EDITOR'S FOREWORD

What motivated ordinary men and women in our century to resist tyranny was something which truly intrigued me when I saw the first German soldiers marching through my native Hungary in 1941. I was interested not only in the actual act of resistance but also in why the people did what they did. I found during those days something very uplifting and hopeful about men and women who were willing to sacrifice their lives so that others might live in a better society. I remember still the impact made on my adolescent mind when a journalist who throughout his life had worked for a Right-wing paper in my home town suddenly decided to print posters bearing the slogan 'National Socialism is Death'. These subsequently appeared all over town. The idea occurred to him while he was shaving one morning. He stood in front of the mirror, he said, and suddenly saw his face in a way in which he had never seen it before. He said it was the face of a traitor. The face asked him, 'What are you going to do about this? What are you going to do about the injustice that is on its way?' By the time he had finished shaving he was ready with the answer. When everyone had gone home that night he used his own paper's presses to print the posters and then went out and put them up himself. I think that there is something symbolic in this episode: a man's seeing his face in the mirror and the reflection's speaking to him from the glass. I always hoped that one day, when National Socialism was over, I would be able to gather a number of people together and allow them to speak freely about their fight against tyranny.

The task was a difficult one because I wanted to find 'ordinary' people, not necessarily professional resisters, politicians or the like, but people who at one point had to face their conscience, and then acted, people who subsequently returned to their ordinary everyday lives. To find the famous would have been easy; to find the less known was very difficult.

I wanted to include in this book the accounts of various forms of resistance which have taken place in our century. Thus we have Gisèle Halimi, whose noble work as a lawyer on behalf of those who suffered in the difficult days of the Algerian troubles caused her own arrest and anxious suffering; we have a chapter from South Africa, where Doctor Ungar spoke what he felt as a Rabbi, and so was deported; a chapter by Wolfgang Müller from the German Army itself, because that is a story which is not often told and I wanted to have an account of it in this book. We also have a chapter from the heart of wartime heroism and resistance in Poland by Waclaw Zagorski, and one from Ernest Blythe in Ireland, who can remember the time when resistance was necessary much nearer home. There is also my own chapter, which was added rather under protest, and under pressure from the publisher. I would have preferred something from a coloured writer, but after many invitations, the result was quite negative.

Each story speaks for itself and I believe that each one is of significance today because we live in a world where tyranny is with us still.

The years ahead will be the most crucial for Man's survival since he appeared on this planet half a million years ago: never before has he faced the possibility of global extinction. And never before has he been so near to solving some of his most chronic problems: the chance of a longer, healthier life, freedom from hunger and the possibility of living in peace. Man's growth throughout the millennia is on two levels—the intellectual and the emotional. While he has learned more and more about the nature of the physical world, he has progressed in very small measure, if at all, from the day when his primitive instincts demanded him to kill. He physically exists in a world of science fiction, yet emotionally he is still part of the jungle. Only knowledge of himself will lead him out of this chaos, and only this knowledge will teach him to tolerate others.

If man does survive, he may emerge into the timeless future. One day he will want to look back—to understand the nature of the change which contributed to his survival—he will want to know what happened in our present day and age. Beyond the wars, dictatorships, revolutions and brutality, he will observe an area of human life which contributed to his own survival. The question of what motivated men and women to defy the power of tyrants should be of particular interest to him; the history of darkness is also the history of light.

Resistance against tyranny is not, however, something that should concern only our great-great-grandchildren. It is something that *we* should be concerned about because, apart from the great evils of tyranny in our world, there are other evils manifesting themselves in our societies: the power of institutions, churches and tradition. Society's demand for conformity is but another aspect of tyranny. We still harbour great prejudices against those who rebel against conformity, and we reject them. We still are ready to crucify those whose vision of a better world is different from our own.

Tyranny, it seems, begins as silence; one begins to tolerate intolerance. Then one feels guilty about the silence. And when the next stage comes, it is difficult to break the silence as it is dangerous to do so. It is a different silence now. It is ruled by fear. Now one becomes a participant in tyranny whether one wants to or not.

It seems that it is easier to resist if one is the target of the tyrant; it is more difficult if others are involved. I often ask myself whether, if I had been born in National Socialist Germany, brought up to hate, I would have, or could have, resisted. The true, tragic answer is 'No'. Thus anyone who did resist in National Socialist Germany deserves genuine homage: he has shown an ability to be free from the forces of gravity in his own environment.

It is relevant to notice at what point one begins to rebel. Resistance against a tyrant at one point in time may be less noble than at another—we have examples here.

I often wonder how many people who take part in protest marches in the United States are truly the friends of the Negroes and how many are merely trying to work something out of their systems which has little to do with the Negro question; how many are truly zealous?; how many act with intellectual integrity?; how many with common sense?; how many do it because of a combination of factors? It seems to me that it does not really matter what the personal motives are if, in the end, resistance against tyranny is successful. Can we expect imperfect human beings to carry out perfect human acts?

EUGENE HEIMLER

TUNISIA AND ALGERIA

Gisèle Halimi

It is not always easy to understand just what are the original impulses which are later to govern the rest of one's life. Often the first indications of them pass almost unnoticed and a great deal must happen before they are confirmed and the whole design takes shape. I am trying to find my way back to these first feelings.

I think that for me everything began one evening in 1944, with a completely unexpected fit of anger from my father. I was already seventeen and beginning my philosophy studies. We were spending our holidays at Carthage, near the sea. As in other years, I had joined up with the young friends with whom I played every summer, Hedi and Skander. Their luxurious villa stood next to our more modest one. All my childhood seems bound up in the games on the beach, and in the smooth, enveloping sea. We seemed part of one family and our games were a natural, happy reaction to this country of bright colours, scents and sparkling light.

On this particular day, after a mock battle on the rocks, the boys suggested a climb up the ruins of Gammarth by moonlight. Everybody was enthusiastic. We decided to meet after dinner with our bicycles, in the outhouses we shared.

My sister and I were just about to leave when my father suddenly appeared, looking angry. He wanted to know who we were going with on the expedition. The names of Hedi and Skander seemed to trigger off his pent-up rage. 'It is time you understood, both of you. . . .' What on earth had we done now? 'You are no longer children. . . .' Soon he gave the astounding order, 'As from today, I forbid you to go about with those boys'. He added, 'Those street-Arabs, those lousy devils', and when I tried to argue with him— 'A tart is more respected than one of our girls who goes about with Arabs.'

That night, the bicycles remained neatly in the outhouse. I could not get to sleep. I tossed and turned in my bed, a prey to some deep, undefined disturbance of the mind. 'Street-Arabs . . . lousy'—Skander and Hedi *could not be* street-Arabs, because we had always known them. One day, we all knew, Hedi would take his father's place. In his turn he would collect taxes, mete out justice, exert his authority as regional administrator. Skander would, perhaps, study law, or medicine. For the moment he was apathetically attending classes at the French lycée, and he had just joined the Yacht Club. Were these friends of mine street-Arabs? In the end, sleep overcame me at dawn. I woke up late in the morning, my face streaked with tears.

For the first time, the nature of racial prejudice had been shown to me. The blow had hit me the harder because it had come from my adored father. No doubt, the wound itself had been made in various ways, the separation from my playmates being only the outward sign of this deeper separation. Anyhow, that night, for the first time in my life, I recognised irreparable injustice. The next day, I knew that my childhood was over.

It was at this time that my parents tried to arrange a marriage for me. I was seventeen. 'Women age quickly . . . women need security. Women are born for home-making.' What else can I say? My mother, in repeating these hackneyed phrases to me, only wanted my good. I knew that. At my age, she herself had already had a son—my elder brother. It was high time that I forgot my scandalous expeditions with the local boys and behaved myself properly.

There was a man who had asked for my hand. He was young (thirty-five!), rich (an oil merchant!). In short, he pleased my mother, and she said I pleased him. This episode seemed to me so unreal that, at the time, I felt I was playing some new game, only this time one in which grown-up people took part. But I soon realised that a whole system of social machinery was being put into operation. I would have to take care of my clothes, I would have to give up playing on the beach, I would have to. . . . The idea overwhelmed me one evening when my mother told me about my 'intended's' next visit.

I asked sharply, 'And my studies?'

My mother seemed nonplussed. 'What studies?'

A fierce argument followed, in which I said suddenly—without really having thought about it—that I wanted to be a barrister and I would study law in Paris. This remark seemed so far-fetched at the time, that it provoked no argument. My mother said simply, 'In the meantime, you are going to get married.'

In June, I passed the second half of my philosophy baccalauréat with honours. At the same time, my elder brother failed his first law examination. His failure made my parents so angry that, in all the fuss, my own success went entirely unnoticed.

Just like that evening not so long before, when, for the first time, my father had seemed so unjust that from one moment to the next he became a stranger to me, I had the feeling again that some link had broken between me and my family. But this time I did not want to cry. I was controlled, my mind sharp. And, strangely, I thought, 'I am on Skander's side this time, I am like him.'

Now, these things seem absolutely clear to me. But in the Tunisia in which I lived then, contempt for Arabs and contempt for women did not appear to have any clear connection. If the Jews despised the Arabs, the Arabs in their turn despised them, and the women of both communities led more or less the same life.

What is obvious to me today is that, in the deep foundations of this society based on autocratic ideas, could be found ignorance, poverty (greater or less), atavisitic intolerance (carefully preserved), and the contemptible rivalry of the oppressed groups. All were equally victims of the same disease: colonialism. From ever-present family oppression, to political tyranny, the distance was nothing, that is to say, there was no distance. Liberty only implies one step, because it is first and foremost understanding for all.

It was not easy to leave Tunisia at that time. The war was hardly over. Communications with France remained difficult. After a struggle, I succeeded in getting a special pass which gave me

3

the right to a place on a military aircraft. Eight days later, I was in Paris, enrolled in the Law Faculty at the Sorbonne. In my passion of happiness, I would willingly have enrolled myself in ten other Faculties if the time-tables of these various courses had not clashed.

§

I stayed three years in Paris. I haunted libraries, went to concerts, spent hours in museums. I rushed from theatres to cinema-clubs, from cinema-clubs to art galleries. . . . My intellectual curiosity seemed to have no end.

Friends had helped me find accommodation. I had gone to live in Clichy, with a working-class couple who rented me a small room in their tiny apartment. The man was an active member of the Left Wing, who told me ten times a day that I was like a daughter to him and I could count on him whatever happened. I had arrived in Paris with some oil and green coffee. This treasure, everyone had said, would make me accepted much more easily. When I had settled into the home of these good people who showed me so much verbal affection, I made them a present of my cans of oil and my bag of coffee. Their pleasure was a joy to see. But it lasted as short a time as their gratitude. When the provisions were used up, they made me understand that I must get some more. For that, I had to write to my parents. My self-respect prevented me. My landlord, who could not understand my scruples, soon blamed me for my ingratitude. The situation deteriorated rapidly. One evening, this left-wing supporter called me a 'dirty Jew'. I packed my case and left at once.

I was amazed. I had always been sure, like a sort of gnomic truth, that the French people were without racial prejudice. It was a terrible awakening for me. While asking the local shopkeepers in the area for a room, I thought of my father. He treated the Arabs like dirt and prided himself on the respect the French showed him. But here in France, I, his daughter had been treated like an Arab. I was a 'dirty Jew'. There were certain French people who said to their children, 'Don't go about with Jews; they're lousy'.

The term had started. I worked very hard, and soon I found myself part of a group of young people who were doing the same work. I was good friends with them and we spent whole nights arguing passionately. But probably I became over-excited when

4

the conversation was about women, their rights and the difficulties they must unceasingly try to overcome, because in these conversations, my friends took fright easily, changed the subject or saved themselves with a joke. 'Ah, no doubt,' they said, 'in your country. . . .' They wanted to be nice and make me understand that, coming from where I did, my background was, nevertheless, to be respected, and the things I said were excusable.

These understatements, reservations, false condescensions, disgusted me. When someone told me one evening that I had an 'exotic charm' I wanted to slap his face.

They were not free either, these offshoots of Montaigne, Voltaire and Diderot. . . . There was a long way to go for all of us.

In the June examinations, I passed my first law exams and got two certificates in philosophy. The next year I got the same results. . . . The third year, I graduated in law and gained the certificate giving me the right to practise as a barrister.

I considered enrolling myself for my period of apprenticeship at the Bar in Paris. But during the previous months my health had not been good, and a doctor friend advised me to spend a time in my native sunshine.

So it was that I went back to Tunisia.

§

'The right to take life' was the subject suggested that year at the trial of oratory for young barristers in Tunis. I had got off the boat a week before the date fixed for the carrying out of this test. From the start, it seemed obvious that I had not got a chance. In this Tunisia of the Protectorat, it was just as difficult for a young girl to get one of the first places as for an Arab. The meeting took place in the presence of official representatives of the Resident-General and of His Highness, the Bey. Many very important officials were also there. In this provincial setting, the oratorical contest was obviously rather a fashionable event.

For me to make a frontal attack on this noble gathering seemed sheer foolhardiness, for they would judge me mercilessly for my twofold cheek—as a woman and as a 'native'.

I have read my notes again today. In a few minutes I referred to Saint Luke, Spinoza, Schopenhauer. Later I spoke of Kant, Leibnitz, St. Thomas Aquinas. . . . Then came Nietsche, Hegel, Joseph de Maistre, Auguste Comte. At the end of quarter of an hour, the applause paid tribute to the breadth of my culture.

5

I remember that I also launched a violent attack against the 'western' war. I said that, stifled by his superiors, the soldier became a robot and it therefore must be asked what was the meaning of phrases like 'human dignity', or 'respect for the individual'. I scourged those who had dropped the atomic bomb on Japan and denounced the mystique of militarism. I ended by saying that to recognise the right to kill was to open the door to evil instincts, to give free range to perverted appetites and incite megalomania.

After a short discussion, the judges proclaimed me laureate of the contest. I had won. I was very happy.

An apparently liberal law united French and Tunisian barristers in the same professional body in Tunis. But one did not have to be very shrewd to spot the endless antagonisms which seethed beneath this legal cover. It had always been the rule that the President of the Bar and the President of the Union of Young Barristers should both be of French nationality. No document supported this unfair bias. But 'the custom' was savagely upheld.

It was exactly at the time of the election of the President of the Union of Young Barristers that we decided to wage war. We put up our own candidate, Hedi K., against the traditional French ones. He was a young colleague full of professional talent, deserving more than anyone to be elected. Nevertheless, he had the double disadvantages of being Tunisian and a Nationalist. His candidature was the threat of the native wolf going into the sheepfold of the Protectorat.

The campaign was fought with violent feeling. Among the young intellectuals, the arguments put forward were often much the same as those of the 'colons'. We were told that the Arabs were neither capable of governing themselves, nor of building a nation. Certainly, some Muslim colleagues had real qualities. But they must be led and directed. For a long time they would only be clever inferiors.

With a very small majority, Hedi K., was elected. I was elected Vice-President. Our stubbornness was obviously not the only reason for this victory. Fundamental political changes were taking place throughout the country. They had certainly affected the outcome of the election.

A new Resident had been appointed in Tunisia, an Admiral. He arrived in the bay of Tunis in a cruiser. The reason for this dramatic appearance was only too obvious. France was playing at intimidation. After that, the use of force became inevitable.

Some days after the war-like Admiral had settled in, the first explosions made Tunisia into a country in open revolt. Martial law was proclaimed, and people were arrested quite arbitrarily. In revenge, the explosions increased in number. The 'legality' of the Protectorat soon found itself powerless faced with this situation. Laws to enforce a state of emergency were hastily drawn up.

Military Tribunals were soon being held ceaselessly. Batches of suspects, arrested in the morning, were condemned in the evening, after a barrister appointed to this duty had muttered a few useless words from a brief he did not know.

It was becoming more and more urgent to organise a defence for the militant nationalists. One of our Tunisian colleagues took on the job. I let him know that he could count on me. It seems to me now that I had always been ready to commit myself to this cause.

The first briefs given to me reinforced my determination. Was it possible that they could arrest men on such scanty grounds, that they dared keep them so long in the hands of the police without any legal protection, above all submit them to such brutalities?

In the prison where I went to see these 'dangerous terrorists', I usually found very reasonable men who laughed at the fears I had for them. Putting aside the brief which I wanted to discuss with them, they questioned me avidly about what was going on 'outside', the number of incidents, the reactions of the people. Anxiously, they asked me, too, for the names of those who had been arrested most recently.

One morning, I received a telephone call from the acting President of the Bar. He was astonished that I was not falling in line with my women colleagues in Tunis who wanted to be relieved of appearing before the Military Tribunals. This veiled request, which I ignored, shocked me deeply. I thought such action would be cowardly and contrary to all our efforts. I told the President that there was no question for me of ceasing to plead for the Nationalists.

The sessions of the Military Tribunals now occupied the greater part of my day. Without much hope, we struggled to limit the hardships of the repression. After a sentence which was too heavy, it was the condemned themselves who most often gave us back

7

our confidence. Before that time, I had never known such men careless of their own lives, inspired by their beliefs. By knowing them, I had, at last, the feeling of being able to distinguish what was essential to life and what was of no importance.

I was becoming a better person.

A little later, the administration having given up all pretence of operating legally, our Tunisian colleagues were deported to the South. We heard that their health was sorely tried by the climate, hot days and freezing nights, and by the hygienically deplorable conditions in which they were forced to live.

At the end of a stormy debate, the Executive Committee of the Union of Young Barristers voted for a motion drawing the attention of the public powers to the plight of the barristers who had been deported. The newspapers took the matter up. Our initiative was reproved. Before long, the Bar Council, that model of submissiveness, criticized us severely.

But the situation developed irrevocably. Everyone knows the stages which marked the progress of Tunisian independence. In December, 1952, the famous Trade Union leader, Ferhat Hached, was killed by the bullets of the colons. His assassination inflamed both sides. In September, 1953, Admiral de Hautecloque was recalled to Paris. His successor, Voizard, strengthened the repressive measures even more. Immersed in Viet-Nam, the French government hesitated before fighting on several fronts at once. Dien-Bien-Phu gave the death knell to French Colonialism. In July, 1954, Bourguiba, deported to the Ile de Groix, was put in enforced residence in the Loiret, not far from Paris. There my colleague, Y.D., and I, were among the first to visit him. At the end of July, the new Prime Minister, Pierre Mendès-France, arrived in Tunisia and on the 31st internal self-government was proclaimed.

All these events, which I had lived to the full, marked me deeply. Up till then, my ideas had been above all things moral. I dreamed of a free world and brotherly love because this was in keeping with my humanist ideals. But I had not considered the means necessary to make my dreams reality.

The struggle of the Tunisian 'fellaghas' opened my eyes. I had been hurled into a world of violence, deception, and lies. At the same time, I had learned to recognise modest courage, endless disinterestedness, the daily heroism of ordinary people. The realisation of ideals was by way of torture, blood and shame.

8

The usurpers would never voluntarily give up their privileges. They would always have to be wrested away by force. Any other way was only a temporary measure, a further alienation. I hated that this had to be; but no choice seemed open. A rebel or an accomplice of the oppressor, there was no other way.

So my convictions became deeper, ever more consistent. From being a moral point of view, they developed into a political conscience. . . .

§

At dawn on the 1st November, 1954, revolution broke out in Algeria. This new uprising stupefied even the most progressive circles. In spite of the conciliatory gestures from the Ministry of the Interior in Paris, the four simultaneous attacks, in four parts of the country, proved that this was definitely a very serious movement, carefully prepared and remarkably well carried out. The gravity of the situation did not escape the colonialists. So a policy of unheard-of repressions was quickly put into force.

Special powers were granted to the French Government for the first time in March 1955, and again in March 1956. These measures bound Algeria in chains and made all acts of resistance illegal.

I had been living in Paris for some months. Together with some colleagues—and how few we were to begin with—I began to collect briefs, each word of which was written in blood.

For those of us who had lived through the repression in Tunisia the past seemed tame compared with what was happening now. The brutal impositions of the security forces in Algeria were beyond belief. In the prisons, the stories of the rebels froze us with horror. In a few weeks we came to know all the infamous means which were used, for eight years, in an attempt at pacification—blows, electric shocks, total immersion in baths of cold water, hanging, rape, to name only a few.

I believe it would be true to say that eighty per cent of the Algerians arrested for one reason or another between 1954 and 1962, were tortured. 'Some isolated cases', M. Pineau had said at U.N.O. where he represented France. Each day, at that time, our notebooks were full of the names of 'missing persons', suspects being given third-degree treatment, so-called 'suicides' who were actually finished off by the parachutists because they were no longer in a fit state to be tried. There were innocent people struck down from behind when they tried to get away after a pretence liberation.

9

The entire Algerian people was becoming no more than a living sore.

At this time, I went to Algeria at least once a week. In fact, I spent my life there. My stays in Paris between two trips were only to collect information, to try to rouse the interest of liberal-minded people, influential people, who were close to those in power.

Once when I went to the Palais de Justice to see the Bar President on business, I came across some of my colleagues. Their days were full of divorce cases, business meetings, smart dinners. . . . This soft, sophisticated atmosphere seemed unbearable to me. I was in a hurry to be back in the interviewing rooms at the prisons of Barberousse or Maison-Carrée. It seemed to me that all the dignity in the world was to be found in the faces of these underfed humiliated rebels, who still bore the marks of blows.

But in Algiers, in Bône, in Oran, even getting out of an aeroplane, the war weighed me down. I knew that again I must live for five or six days with nerves strained to breaking point, and aching heart, sick with shame and disgust.

For eight years Algeria could only be this leaden weight dragging me down as I went on my well-trodden way from the Airport to the Tribunal, from the Tribunal to the prisons. And the only faces I can keep in my mind of that time are those of the men whose very lives we were often trying to save, and whose honour we were always trying to defend.

I remember particularly the face of a young peasant for whom I had to plead one morning in Constantine.

Taken in the maquis, armed, he had hardly spoken during the preparation of his brief. He just went on repeating, 'There was nothing else I could have done. . . .'

At the hearing, many incidents made me clash with the Presiding Judge, a Colonel who wanted to finish off as quickly as possible a case which ordinarily would have presented no problems. All the members of the maquis carrying arms were condemned to death. Nevertheless, I insisted that certain aspects of my client's case must be interpreted. The Judge and the interpreter exchanged exasperated glances. I have written down here, from memory, the extraordinary dialogue which followed.

'Will you ask the accused what he did before the rebellion?'

'I was an agricultural labourer.'

'How much did he earn each day?'

(Here, there was a new development. The Presiding Judge refused to put the question, maintaining it had no relevance to the accusation. The question was put, however, but the interpreter pretended not to understand the accused's answer. As I understand Arabic, I had to interpret.)

'My client wants to say that he worked for board and lodging, without being paid at all.'

'No other questions?'

'No other questions, M. le Président. Here is a man who worked for twelve hours a day and was never paid. . . .'

The Judge turned towards the accused. 'Have you anything to say?'

The accused rose to his feet. He was terrifyingly thin. A tattered shirt hung over his faded trousers. This was obviously the first time he had spoken in public. He hesitated and began at last:—

'I must tell you . . . yes . . . I could not have done anything else. I don't know anything about politics. I worked on a Frenchman's estate, in the vineyard. One had to get up very early in the morning and by evening the work was never finished. I ate. In winter I slept in a shed and, in good weather, out of doors. . . . Sometimes my master came round and gave out cigarettes. . . .' He thought a minute and then went on:

'There were some men who went away one day. They said, "We will get rid of all the French." But I stayed behind. I ate. But at night I knew that those men came down from the mountain again to get more food. I heard them.'

The judge wanted to interrupt the accused. I protested. Ignoring the noise the young rebel went on, 'One night, they came. They gave me a gun and they said, "Now, you must come up the mountain. You must come with your brothers." I took the gun. It was a good gun. I said, "I will come. . . . I will go with my brothers".'

The military judges were suddenly paying close attention.

'They spoke of the independence of Algeria. The barrister from Paris will talk to you about independence. As for me, I took the gun and went. I felt something had happened to me . . . I said to myself, "Your brothers have come for you, they need you." Before that I was no use; I was an Arab, a peasant, and now I was a man. I went up the mountain and I said to myself, "Now you are a man. . . ." Afterwards, I realised I could be arrested, condemned.

I knew that I could be executed. And today you are going to execute me, but that doesn't matter. . . . My brothers needed me and nothing else matters.'

He tried to add something. Then he simply repeated, 'That's all, nothing else matters'.

An hour later, the Tribunal passed its verdict. The young rebel was condemned to forced labour for life. By his dignity, he had won the admiration of his judges and not one of them had dared to condemn him to death.

In other cases, 'justice' completed the work of the torturers. In December 1956, when Amédée Froger, President of the Association of the Mayors of Algeria was assassinated, bloody reprisals were carried out by the European extremists. These were the first manhunts. Dozens of Muslims, shot down haphazard in the streets, paid for a crime that the F.L.N. had not perhaps committed. Whatever the truth, a 'suspect' appeared before the examining magistrate as Froger's assassin. I was there to take part in his defence. The accused pleaded 'not guilty'. I was convinced that he was definitely innocent. At the same time several other Algerians, submitted to inhuman torture, had also 'admitted' that they were the assassins. In the case of such confusion, judges anxious for the truth would have tried to get more information, or given a verdict of 'not proven'.

My client appeared before the Military Tribunal. During the hearing, it came out that Froger's probable assassin had a long scar on one of his legs. This fact became important evidence. I was able to declare that the accused had no trace of a wound. This was definite. Nevertheless, capital punishment was passed on my client. The letters he wrote to me from the condemned cell, bore witness to the confidence he had in French justice to the end. One day, he thought, they would recognise their mistake. I went to see him the evening before his execution. The Prison Authorities did not see fit to inform me that his appeal for mercy had been rejected. It was only when I got back to Paris the next day that I found out from the newspapers that my client had been guillotined.

Today, the reawakening of these memories overwhelms me. Again I experience the blind rage, the stifling feeling of powerlessness. Again I see the suffering faces, hear the grave words. How could such atrocities have gone on for so long without provoking a vast wave of indignation which would have swept away those petty officials of crime, those inferior butchers, in an instant? And how, after such things, can similar situations arise in the world, at the moment when I am writing this, or when others read it?

§

On 10th May, 1958, I took the plane for Algiers again. I had realised in advance that my stay this time would be short, because, as well as a case to plead before the Military Tribunals, I had only to act on behalf of three rebels in various preliminary hearings. Algiers looked as usual; patrols, barbed-wire barricades, the usual anonymous crowds of people. Rumour had it that the F.L.N. had shot three French prisoners. I went to the Tribunal to work on the brief I had to plead.

The next day *Dimanche Matin*, the most reactionary newspaper in Algiers, published an appeal from its Director, Alain de Sérigny, to General de Gaulle. Deep in the notes for my plea for the defence, I did not pay much attention to this strange article. In the evening a colleague from Paris who had been in Algiers for some days and had to go back to France urgently, telephoned me to ask me to take his place in a case which would be called before the Military Tribunal in two days. I accepted. Taking his place simply meant that my permit to stay would have to be extended by twenty-four hours.

On Monday, 12th May, I pleaded my case at the end of the morning, as expected. My client, who was only accused of collecting funds for the F.L.N. got off with five years in prison, which was a comparatively light sentence. In the afternoon I found out that the demonstration that the Ex-service Men had planned for the 13th, as a protest against the execution of the French prisoners, had been forbidden by Lacoste, the Cabinet Minister who had been specially appointed to run the country. Instead, a placing of wreaths would take place at the War Memorial.

Therefore, on the 13th, when I came out of the Military Tribunal I made a detour round by the Forum. An enormous crowd had overrun the terraced gardens which rose as far as the Government building. This wild mob shouted various slogans, among which I made out, 'Death to Bourguiba', and another which demanded the destruction of the Palais-Bourbon. At the same time, car drivers stuck in the crowd, sounded the three short notes and two long of 'Al-gé-rie Fran-çaise . . . Al-gé-rie Fran-çaise' on their horns.

Suddenly a great ovation drowned all the shouting, then a

13

chanted slogan came closer and closer until it reached the place where I was standing. Finally I made out 'SOUSTELLE . . . SOUSTELLE . . . SOUSTELLE . . .' I was amazed. Someone accosted me rudely. I turned round. An employee of the record office of the Military Tribunal, who had recognised me shouted, 'If I have any advice to give you it is to get away from here quickly'. He added, 'You and the Arabs, it's all over'.

I went off with a group of people and back to my hotel. During the whole evening the streets were full of groups of hysterical young people shouting 'Algérie française', but also 'Put Massu in power', and 'Long live Soustelle'. From time to time, bursts of gun fire came from the higher parts of the town.

I went to the balcony of my room. A young fanatic, beside himself, caught sight of me and shouted in my direction, shaking his fist, 'Algiers will save France'. All night I was kept awake by shots, yells and the hooting of cars. At dawn, I telephoned P.B., another colleague from Paris whom I knew to be in Algiers. He thought the situation very dangerous and intended going back to France that very night. We decided to meet in the hotel in the early afternoon.

I spent the morning at the Military Tribunal. When I met P.B., he told me that all flights out of Algiers had been cancelled. A Committee of Public Safety had 'taken over power' in the Algiers' Government headquarters. Salan and Massu were on the side of the uprising. They were waiting for Soustelle, who was to head the movement. Time was running out. P.B. thought that in staying a few more hours in Algiers, we risked being arrested and even executed. We found out that a boat called the *Kairouan* was on the point of leaving for Marseilles. Hastily, we got ready to go. A few minutes later we were on board.

Four hours went by. The boat stayed at the quayside. There was a lot of confusion on the pier where some parachute officers were arguing fiercely with members of the crew. After a while, the officers came on board by a rope gangway. By megaphone, a voice commanded all the passengers to go on to the pier; the officers were about to carry out an identity check. When our turn came to show our papers, some soldiers came forward. A captain told P.B. and me that we were under arrest. We were quickly put ashore and taken to a covered lorry which was parked at the entrance to the port.

'Why are we being arrested?'

'Orders', an officer told me, laconically.

I refused to get into the lorry. Some marines pushed me in forcibly, tearing my dress.

We went along the coast road, above the sea. P.B. leaned towards me and murmured, 'They are going to shoot us'. I looked at him, he was very pale. I said—to reassure myself—'They don't shoot barristers as easily as that'. He shrugged his shoulders, 'Then why have they arrested us?' There did not seem to be any answer. I told myself, 'This time, it's all over'. It seemed strange.

The lorry stopped. I looked out through a hole in the tarpaulin. We had come to the Casino de la Corniche; for several months it had been the 'sorting depot', that is, the place of torture. We had been told by a lot of our clients about the workings of this sinister spot. Therefore, we had no illusions about our fate.

Suddenly, there were shouts. Then we saw a sort of jointless puppet, his face horribly swollen which two parachutists were dragging by the shoulders. The group walked in front of the lorry. A few minutes later, the soldiers made us get out and took us to the first floor of the Casino. On the landing, two guards took P.B. down one corridor, while two others pushed me in the opposite direction. At the end of the corridor my guards opened the door of a little room which, at first glance, might have been a kitchen. They locked me in. I looked round me. Some electric cords hung down, a water tap had been placed just above a marble table of strange proportions; some cords were tied to a nail in the wall. There was no possible doubt. I was in a torture chamber.

Two or three hours went by, during which, in a state of horror, I could not keep my eyes off the instruments of torture. Later, a woman came in to search me. She asked me what I had done. I said I was a barrister and I had defended Algerians. Her face hardened. She had taken my scarf and thrown on to it my pens, my bag and my papers. I begged her to leave me the snapshots of my sons. She refused roughly. When she had finished searching, she tied up all the things in my scarf and seemed ready to go. Then she changed her mind and said harshly:—

'Your little boys—you would have done better to think of them than defend murderers.'

Alone again, I tried to work out the time. We had been arrested at four o'clock. That must have been four or five hours ago. Was it really so late? I told myself, 'They will do *that* tomorrow . . . now it is too late. At least for tonight.'

I had defended murderers. I had written articles, spoken at

public meetings. Everywhere I went, I had denounced the use of violence with all my strength. Now they had me. I imagined them setting on me, making me pay for each defence, each action, each meeting. 'You are going to see, my pretty. You will feel the torture bath, the club, the electric shock. You have not spoken for nothing.'

A strange feeling ran through me. A sort of slight trembling, a queer spasm which I could not control. Little by little it became stronger. I shook, I was frightened. I could no longer understand the importance of what I had felt to be so important. I had been wrong. The policewoman was right. I had children; since I had been separated from their father, I was entirely responsible for them. I ought to have thought of that. Hadn't my mother often said, 'It is wicked to run such risks when one has children'. Why had I wanted to do the impossible, be a mother like other women, but also be a woman with a profession, political convictions and a desire to act? I would have done better to live quietly, plead divorce cases during the day and listen to records in the evening. I would die. I would disappear and no one would know what I had thought in this pretence kitchen, far away from my own people in my last moments.

A cry made me jump . . . a long cry, tearing, inhuman . . . the cry of a wounded animal. It was P.B. I was sure I knew his voice. They had begun on him. They questioned his flesh with their steel instruments. Soon they would come for me.

Then I shouted, 'Stop, murderers, stop'.

Surprised, but prompt, my guards opened the door and leaped at me. 'What is the matter with you?'

I struggled, I tried to hit them. 'Murderers, you are torturing Pierre. Murderers.'

Amazed, they let me go. 'My God', said one of them wide-eyed, 'this barrister of the "fellaghas" is absolutely mad.'

Actually, it was not P.B. who had shouted. Not him, not anyone. He told me so later. And a few minutes after this aural hallucination when they took me down to the cell where I was to spend the night, I was able to glimpse him, through an open door, his shadow reflected, peacefully asleep on his camp bed.

The arrival of the guards had put an end to my nightmare. I sat on a stool and said to myself, 'This stool will be used by the torturers'. But already my agony of mind had lessened. I thought, 'Anyway, I could not have lived otherwise,' and again, 'To have

16

lived otherwise would have been to shut my eyes to the world around me.' But words echoed in my mind. The guards had left the door open. I could see the foot of one of them on which he rested his weight. I was reassured. Two lines of Eluard came back to me.' 'Il n'y a qu'une vie—C'est donc qu'elle est parfaite.' I understood the words. A man must live, it is only through living that he can realise himself completely. I had filled my life well, with the sun in Carthage, the books I had read, my sons, and what my profession had allowed me to do for others. Others had done as I had done, others would do so again. I could die.

But how could I get near the window without making my guards suspicious? Three steps. Then open the window, pull myself up, throw myself into space. The sea beat at the foot of the cliffs. The familiar sea of childhood. In getting up from my stool, I made a very slight noise. A guard looked in, gave me a sleepy glance and disappeared. I jumped up, rushed the window, put out my hand . . .

A couple of sharp blows made me stagger. The catch of the window which I had caught hold of, seemed to fade and waver. A rough voice shouted:

'Don't move, do you hear, no more tricks.'

I opened my eyes. I was lying on the floor. My guards leaned over me, seized my shoulders and propped me against the wall. I caught a few words:—

'Of all the crazy creatures.'

'What a business.'

'They ought to do something with her. I am fed up.'

A little later, a baby-faced police sergeant came into the room. He ordered me to follow him. I got up painfully. I wanted to know where he was taking me. He gave a lively wink to the corporal who was with him:

'Sleep . . . that suit you?'

I was on my guard. Still, the idea of being taken by the gendarmes seemed to me a good omen. We went back the other way down the long corridor on the first floor. I saw P.B. The sight of him comforted me. I tried to ask some questions. What had they done with my suitcase? I would need my night things to go to bed. The sergeant answered enigmatically that it would follow. In spite of the terror that knotted my insides, I pretended to be hungry. He said, 'That hasn't been allowed for.' We came out finally at the end of another corridor. The sergeant made me go into a cell measuring about three metres square. It had no furniture and no window. A flattened mattress was spread out on the floor, which glistened with damp.

'Try to sleep all the same', said the sergeant.

The door shut again. I heard the metallic noise of the lock. Night overwhelmed me. I thought of all sorts of possibilities. If the parachutists had handed me over to the police, was this a sign that civil law was in force again? But if this were so, why didn't they let us go? Perhaps Soustelle had been successful in Paris. Then, perhaps we would not be executed, but tried and condemned to prison for life.

But it was useless to go over and over things like that. One must hold out, try to behave normally. I ran my hands through my hair, in an attempt to brush it. Then I took off my shoes and lay down on the mattress. I could hear confused noises through the door. Echoes of arguments taking place at a distance. At one time, a voice became clearer. I heard, 'This F.L.N. tart . . . against a wall. I tell you, against a wall." I held my breath. My life depended on the mood of one of these unseen speakers, *pieds-noirs* (white settlers), I was certain. I recognised the accent. Another voice said quietly, 'Calm down, Maurice, calm down.' Worn out with emotion, I fell asleep almost immediately.

The sound of keys . . . the creaking of the door . . . I opened my eyes. The police sergeant was carrying an enormous jug, the corporal held out an aluminium can to me. A faint smell of coffee. The smell of life regained.

It was hot and sweet. I drank so greedily that my jailers exchanged amused glances.

'Tell me . . .'

'I know nothing', cut in the sergeant, but without anger. 'The Commandant is coming to see you.'

'And my colleague . . .'

'Don't know,' The door was already shut.

In the morning, I was taken to the basement for questioning. A man in civilian clothes, with a strong southern accent, began to read out some papers in a loud voice. To begin with I could not understand them properly. There was the question of the struggle of the Algerian people, of the validity of this struggle, of the hideous face of torture, the foolishness of racialism. Some phrases seemed familiar to me. At the beginning of this strange reading, I thought, 'they are trying to provoke me.' Then I wondered where I had read all this before. Then suddenly I thought, 'But these are my briefs. These are my notes for the court.'

The swarthy little man looked up from his papers. 'Do you want me to go on?'

Suddenly I was in a gay mood. I said, 'I found it very good.'

'Are you trying to make fun of me?' Furiously he crumpled the pile of documents. 'Slut . . . it is your filth I am reading. This is all the rubbish you produced for your wretches.'

He stood up and shouted insults into my face. I thought he was going to hit me. 'I didn't recognise my own words, but I approve of them.'

The man's anger suddenly abated. Probably he was a good actor and had been trying to intimidate me. He sat down again and dictated. I signed the statement.

We went on to the ceremony of taking finger prints. Looking at my fingers covered in ink, I thought of something which cheered me up. 'The fascists will lose all their battles, because they have no sense of humour, or of dialectic.'

Our imprisonment in the Casino de la Corniche lasted about a week. Inside my windowless cell, I was kept in strict solitary confinement. A short walk in the sunlit court was the only event which marked my day.

Three days after my arrest, I showed the Colonel who commanded the depot, a telegram which I accidentally had on me. This telegram came from the President's Residence and told me that M. Coty would receive me on the 18th May to endorse the appeal of one of my Algerian clients who had been condemned to death. I remarked that it was a pity I was prevented, by such arbitrary measures, from obeying the summons of the Head of the Republic.

The Colonel turned the telegram over and over, as if he doubted its authenticity. Then he said, 'Coty? What trick are you trying to play on me?'

'But Colonel, he is the President of the French Republic.'

The Colonel burst out laughing. 'What Republic?' He added seriously, 'All that's over, the Army is in power . . . it will put a little order into this political mess.'

I wanted to argue.

'Your Coty . . . now he counts for nothing. Understand?'

Some days later P.B. and I were transferred to Aïn Taya, 30 kilometres west of Algiers, which had been one of the most beautiful seaside resorts on the Algerian coast before the revolution.

c

In a deserted hotel, strange holiday makers, all constantly watched, passed each other with an absent air. We were absolutely forbidden to speak to each other. At meals, we were seated with our faces to the wall in such a way that everyone had his back to everyone else.

There were some Prefects, some town clerks, a journalist from *Le Monde*. The civil servants under arrest had, for the most part, refused to recognise the authority of the Committees of Public Safety, and remained obstinately faithful to the Republic.

A lieutenant of the C.R.S. (Riot Police) with perfect manners, explained the rules of this strange hotel to us. In addition to all communications being forbidden, we had to leave the doors of our rooms open, as well as the envelopes of the letters we were allowed to write.

Once settled in my room, I began to think up ways of breaking the rules. To have the door open seemed to me particularly unbearable. I began to sing the song of the Partisans very loudly:

'My friend, do you hear the flight of the dense crows over our planes.'

The guard who was on duty outside my room rushed in. 'It is forbidden to talk.'

'I'm not talking, I'm singing.'

He went out, puzzled. I went on singing. Someone moved about in the next room. I heard my neighbour also whistling the song of the Resistance. This went on until the Lieutenant came back. Without any other comment he said to me, 'The point is taken Maître, you can shut your door.'

Our enclosed life became organised. The weather was fine and warm, the silken sea lapped gently at the foot of the building. For some hours we walked up and down on the tiny terrace allotted to us. At night, I heard the friendly, calming waves which rippled softly outside. What had happened to my sons? How had my long absence been explained to them? Had they been ill-treated in Paris, which I believed to be in the hands of the parachutists? I asked the Lieutenant. He refused to tell me anything about the situation outside. He simply said, 'It would be in your interests for De Gaulle to come to power quickly.'

Nevertheless, the idea did not seem to me a very happy one.

We were guarded by the C.R.S. But we soon realised that they themselves were watched over by the parachutists. That was two concentric circles round us, which made flight seem impossible, but which sometimes gave us the feeling that the balance of power was uncertain in Algiers.

There were often brawls among the parachutists. After drinking, they sang Nazi songs, then suddenly threw themselves on each other, knife in hand. One morning after a noisy night, I found some drops of blood, still fresh on the steps of the terrace.

We had no dealings with the parachute officers. A Lieutenant came to talk to me a few times. Once I said to him, 'You will have to let us go one day.'

He hesitated, then he said, 'You could be transferred. During a transfer, there are always a few losses . . . An ambush . . . Attempts to escape. You understand?'

I understood very well. 'One can't enact the Audin affair a hundred times over. If we disappeared, there would be trouble.'

He smiled savagely. 'We are sick of you exhibitionist intellectuals. . . . Queers, tarts, their dirty little ways don't count for anything here. Here we are men. We are doing a man's work. Do you understand?' He was getting excited by his own words. 'The Arabs are like your Paris types, all pansies. I hate the Arabs myself and I've got the courage to say it, I'll get rid of as many as I can. Yesterday I again accounted for three. It's like swatting flies. That's all true.'

He came towards me and, shaping his hands into a cup, he brought them to his lips. 'I'd drink the blood of the stinking Arabs if I could. Just like that, I'd drink it at one gulp.'

Disgusted, I turned my head away. Our voices had attracted the attention of the Lieutenant of the C.R.S.

'Maître . . . are you holding a meeting?'

'With me, she can always try', growled the parachutist.

The Lieutenant looked at him curiously. 'What was she saying to you?'

I broke in drily. 'It was I who was listening to this gentleman. He was telling me how he loved the Arabs. It was he who was pleading for fraternisation.'

The parachutist began to roar again. The Lieutenant smiled. 'No politics', he said evenly, 'it isn't allowed here.' He turned to me. 'I think it's time you went back to your room.'

That night, I could not sleep. I was sickened by hatred. The war had maddened these young men. An endless war, lost before it was begun. Guarded by such lunatics, we could be butchered like beasts from one minute to the next. We must escape. I went to the window. In the shadows, an enlarged silhouette staggered. It was one of our glorious conquerors drowning his sorrows.

Next day, having got up early, I looked at the sea with which I had always been at one. For the first time in my life, my old accomplice seemed alien. How could I have dreamed of escaping when on one side the parachutists mounted guard and on the other, as far as the horizon, the traitress lapped gently?

I heard the footsteps of the C.R.S. Lieutenant in the corridor. As on every other day, he was going to knock at the door, come in and salute. Then the same short conversation:—

'Good morning, Maître, what can I do for you this morning?'

Before I could answer, as on the previous evening, as on every morning, he would go on with a sad smile, 'Freedom, yes, I know, you've told me already. But that I can't give you.'

The Lieutenant knocked. What can I do for you? But his face was grave. I thought, 'Something has happened to the children.' He said, 'I think we are soon going to be able to give you your freedom.'

I jumped up. 'Are we going to be transferred?'

He smiled. 'No, you are going to be really free.' He waited a moment, then solemnly, 'General de Gaulle has agreed to assume power.'

The formalities were dragged out by some hours because of me. I should have been released first, being a woman and a mother. But hearing that P.B. was being kept because he was a communist, I refused to go without him and took the necessary steps. Twenty-four hours later P.B. was released and we were taken to the airport together.

We went through the journey in a sort of dream.

At Orly, the President of the Bar, journalists, colleagues and friends awaited us at the embarkation desk. Out of all these people I had eyes only for my sons, who were waving timidly to me. I tore them out of the crowd and, taking them both in my arms, ran towards the friendly car which took me home.

§

I am writing all this in Paris in the autumn of 1964. Algeria has just celebrated the 10th anniversary of its revolution. This year, I was not able to be present at the already traditional celebrations in Algiers. I was at Rabat, where I was preparing a brief for the progressive students, whose organisation is threatened with dissolution. Its young President is in prison for having upheld his comrades' claims a little too well. He is accused of a threat to state security, and therefore, in principle, liable to the death penalty.

I don't like going over the same ground again. The past is too full of faces I will never see again, familiar faces which suffering, the firing squad, or the guillotine have removed for ever.

From my adolescent revolt against the prejudices of the grown-up world, to my adult conviction, it seems to me that I have never deviated. To resist the first absurdity, the first lie, forces you to self-commitment. It is a demanding force which can never be denied. Sometimes, remembering certain troubles or times when the threat became the reality, I say to myself, paraphrasing the poet, 'And if I had to do it all again, would I?' It seems as though I would never pluck up enough courage again. But here are the briefs which pile up—MOROCCO . . . IRAQ . . . GABON.

Every time, I protest. I say that my boys are growing up, that they need me . . . that I must have time to read, to live a normal life at last. But still *they* are there. They have irrefutable documents, overwhelming evidence. They say, 'Maître, you can't leave our comrades undefended.' And I think, 'And *my* life?' They go on, 'Maître, these are things which humiliate us all.' And so, I take notes, check names, dates. One day I will be in an aeroplane again, a little frightened, because one never knows what may happen at the embarkation desk.

Perhaps one can't do anything else. Perhaps, if I had been in the country that particular Sunday, I would have had the feeling of lying to myself, of doubting my cause. . . . Perhaps one has to experience injustice very young, even violence itself, to feel this irresistible compulsion.

When I fought for Djamila Boupacha,* the young Algerian tortured by sadists, I understood better where my responsibilities as a woman and my professional duties exactly coincided, that they were only varied expressions of the same desire for light and liberty.

I think now and again of that young parachutist lieutenant who wanted to drink the Arabs' blood. What has happened to him? Was he killed in the ranks of the O.A.S.? Is he far away from France? Or does he live a simple daily life among us, as a teacher, a civil servant, a shop-keeper, a good husband, father and friend? He is

* See Gisèle Halimi and Simone de Beauvoir, *Djamila Boupacha*, André Deutsch and Weidenfeld and Nicolson, 1960.

somewhere, in the same life, in the same world as us. Perhaps in childhood he lacked the things which would later make him a proper man.

It is not these people who are in some way deficient, these criminals who are responsible. For them, horror is the only reason for living. Death—which they deal out—which they risk—gives their lives a truth which reassures them.

The true murderers are those who decide ways and means, in Boards of Directors, ministerial antichambers, the corridors of Parliament. They do not often wield the knife themselves. They talk cheerfully in drawing-rooms about abstract painting, or poetry. It is they nevertheless, who are the true enemies of man.

Their type feeds on our indifference, our lack of true knowledge, our cowardice.

They must be unmasked. It is because of them that half humanity still dies of hunger, suffers torture, feels fear and humiliation every day.

SOUTH AFRICA

André Ungar

The spiritual grandeur of man's courage in the face of oppressive evil manifests itself in many ways in the Republic of South Africa. The perennial and universal theme of resistance unfolds itself within the specific and inimitable tones, rhythm and key of the land and the age. In the 1960s the drama of South Africa is reaching its inevitable climax, though its precise date and outcome is not yet discernible. But the three centuries' encounter between colonising exploitative settler and indigenous African culture clearly indicates the direction of matters. Three million whites, prosperous and, among themselves, still willing to play out at least a façade of democratic procedure, attempt to hold away, and push further and further apart and down, twelve million non-white inhabitants of their country. This majority is fourfold and by now consists of thoroughly and irreversibly detribalised Africans, Cape Coloureds and Indians, completely transformed outwardly and inwardly through industrial, educational and religious development. Parallel with the growing rigour and hysteria of white overlordship, there is not only a heightening of resentment, but also of organisation, leadership and purposeful dedication on the part of the deprived. The tension is becoming almost intolerable. It is most pathetic in those instances where it is blandly denied. Also, the African continental setting where the thirty-fifth independent black state has just come into existence, does little to mitigate the starkness of the situation.

By its very nature resistance follows two distinct patterns, both in its origin and forms of expression. On the one hand there is resistance by the non-white population. What makes their opposition typical is the fact that the master race's pretence of democratic procedure does not apply to them, and the circumstance that in struggling against their oppressors they are fighting for their own personal and communal emancipation. On the other hand, the all too few white men who show any manner of resistance are partially protected (and the paradox is obvious) by their pale pigmentation; they, in contrast to the former, are doing what they do clearly against the hostile wall of their own social matrix and, at least in the short run, against their own interests. But some strands of resisting behaviour deserve to be examined separately, and in some detail.

§

My own personal story is not an exceptionally dramatic one. Yet perhaps its very commonplaceness can help focus some characteristics of the South African predicament as well as the more dramatic contours of some others' confrontations.

Late in 1954 I was ordained as rabbi in London and shortly afterwards I accepted an invitation to the pulpit of Temple Israel in Port Elizabeth, South Africa. While there, I found myself involved in the racial conflict. I spoke from my pulpit about matters of such a nature; published a few articles locally and overseas; I had fairly wide social contact with non-whites; I addressed a number of public meetings of protest against apartheid. Near the end of 1956 I was served a deportation order by the Minister of Interior, and at the beginning of 1957 I left the country. I feel that some of the social and psychological aspects of this rather fleeting episode revealed, to me at any rate, strange and important depths. Circumstances also brought me into touch with men and women who embodied types and triumphs of resistance worth examining.

From the distance of a decade it is difficult to recall precisely the subtle shadings of thought and feeling that mottled my mind at that time; God knows it is hard enough to be objective in introspection even at the time of the impact itself. I was twenty-five years old, my doctorate from London University and my rabbinic ordination certificate hardly dry on the paper yet, my daughter just nine months old. During the immediately preceding few years, I had been struggling to complete my training, keep the financial wolf from the door, do justice to a position as Assistant Rabbi with a large congregation, and come to terms with a none too perfect marriage. The invitation to Port Elizabeth seemed to offer a great deal. For one thing, the tension of impending examinations was forever over. I should be in charge of a congregation of my own, given more responsiblity and at the same time be free from the generous but nagging domination of a senior colleague. Material cares would be banished. Perhaps a new setting would put things right between my wife and myself too. There was a great deal of hope. Also pride: the chance to mould a community according to a pattern I considered worth while. Anxiety, too. What if I fail? My personal life would be in the focus of public attention, and what in the grey homogeneity of London could pass unseen would be pinpointed by provincial curiosity in South Africa. Perhaps the type of sermonising I seemed to be successful with in England would fall flat in my new location. Altogether, perhaps I should not measure up to the demands of ultimate leadership; the snotty-nosed kid will be unmasked, laughed at, driven out with eternal ignominy. Yet, on the other hand there was a contrary fear too. I might succeed too well, succumb to the fleshpots, grow flabby and blend into the scenery for the rest of my life. What some considered a promising career would flatten into a dusty, dreary function behind God's back and, equally bad, behind civilisation's back. No theatres, no concerts, no decent libraries—at first I would suffer, later (infinitely more shameful) come to accept it gladly.

There was also some vague, uncertain anticipation of the country's racial and political complexion. I had been following the daily and weekly press in London fairly systematically during my student years. Father Trevor Huddleston's article in *The Observer* I remember shook me up profoundly; I had not imagined that such unashamed racialism could have survived in the world, and especially under the Union Jack. My general attitude towards Negroes had been a naïve one. Until the age of eighteen when I left my native Hungary I had never seen a non-white person in the flesh. It seemed a little suspect, and ludicrous, when I heard that some people were black. Black as boots? Or beetles? Nonsense— maybe a bit sunburnt, that is all. A silly exaggeration. But then, in photographs and films, I did see them. Tarzan films and their like: lithe naked bodies, with grass skirt and spears, boiling missionaries for lunch. If such creatures really existed surely they were hardly human. Then, coming to London, my world became somewhat more polychromatic. I saw Indians and Chinese and Negroes walking up and down the Edgware Road and Gower Street. Then I sat next to them at lectures, in theatres, in cafeterias. We talked, became friends, argued, fought, made up. Pigmentation simply faded away in my awareness. While at first I stared with popping eyes at every coloured person—not in hostility, only in curious incredulity—before long I ceased to notice the difference. It simply didn't matter. Yet, coming to Africa, many of my old questions were revived. Black men may after all be different in their natural environment than when moving along the Strand in King's College blazers with an umbrella and a copy of Sartre as their load. I was hungry for, and a bit scared of, the exoticism of the Dark Continent. And spasmodically jerked by the news of the apartheid régime down there. I wanted to see for myself and, if possible, deny the cheap journalistic distortion of facts—or else, if (hard to believe) they proved true, see what I could do in combating it. To tell the truth, I did have a qualm or two about going at all for these racial reasons. If the reports which blamed the white population for its oppressiveness were accurate, I would be joining that spineless crowd myself by going. To sell out my own ideals, and to risk my own child's growing up as a racist seemed too high a price to pay for vocational advancement and some sightseeing. If, on the other hand, I were to set myself against the dominant pattern, I should inevitably be a flop in my work, and quite possibly bring dire consequences on my wife and child as well. Either way a sobering prospect. But sobriety was rather far removed from my mood just then. I was filled with the excitement of the journey, the honour, the challenge of it all. And if it included, among other good things, a manly fight, all the better. A heady young exuberance and perhaps an innate delight in battle blurred my remaining London days rather pleasingly.

On arrival, too many novel things surrounded me to spare thought for the racial situation. My congregation showed a spontaneous warmth and hospitality that no chilly English middle-class synagogue would ever be capable of—a disarming reception indeed. The physical aspect of matters (parks, gardens, buildings, and homes) was lavish and lovely beyond imagining. My own position appeared to be a much more significant one than I had anticipated. A whirl of social and official engagements took up most of my time. The only Negroes I saw were courteous servants in the homes and colourful figures in the street briefly glimpsed while one drove by. The total aspect of things was relaxed, mellow and quite peaceful and happy. I caught myself a little relieved as well as disappointed that the renowned *bête noire* was a myth. No Loch Ness monster to harpoon. Racial persecution? Some desperate newspapermen's and clergymen's fancy.

After a few weeks, the pleasant surface of things began to crack up; chinks of inconsistency and uneasiness appeared. Through the subdued stylised terminology of the papers, the face of reality began to be discernible. Encounters in the street, in shops and elsewhere became puzzling, then disturbing and soon enough quite outrageous. Out of sheer curiosity at first, I wanted to see where the 'natives' lived. There was a forbidding disapproval in my white friends' features. Nothing to see. Oh, just like any other working-class district in Europe. Or, terribly dangerous. Might get killed. Police would get the wrong idea, and so on and so forth. At last I decided to take the initiative myself and drove my Austin to New Brighton. Then to Korsten. I still don't know what was more heartbreaking: the dreary infinity of tiny grey concrete boxes that was planned and proudly proclaimed by the authorities as the most up-to-date housing project for natives on the whole continent, or the reeking shantytown of packing crates, rusty corrugated iron and draped rags of sacking and newspapers in a sea of dust and mud. And then human contacts grew too, with a couple of whites who knew and cared, and with some Indian, Cape Coloured and African people who could tell me—and much more dramatically, show me—the truth about South Africa. I found that our own genteel white leisure and wealth was a thin veneer over a vast mass of coloured suffering; and that the distinction was artificially created, maintained and, since the Nationalist victory of 1948, deliberately worsened day after day.

A welter of sentiments surged within me as I gradually learned this. I was bitterly ashamed that I had come to Africa at all: I ought to have known, I should not have fallen victim to too cunning enticement and, worse still, to my own greed and ambition

29

and vanity. I was pained as I contemplated my own new neighbours and friends: they were hypocrites, or 'schizophrenics'—so much gentleness and kindness towards me and to one another and such callous uncaring towards the majority of their own countrymen?

There was also a strand of sentiment that shamed me most of all. One part of my being *rejoiced* at what I saw. I delighted in being part of an aristocracy, a privileged *élite*. Back in Hungary I had, as a child, often wondered with envy what it would have felt like to be born the son of a Baron: rich, gentile, a silver spoon in my mouth. Well, here I suddenly found I had it all. Without any effort of my own, I was granted membership in a most select club. And, yes, in a way I liked it, and found it perfectly right. So it must be, I caught something inside me preen, it is the divine and natural order of things. It gave a sense of security, of reassurance, of noble elevation. Perhaps the Indian caste system, and Aldous Huxley's brave new hierarchy, expressed the ultimate wisdom of society. Hurrah for the top dog . . . especially as I too am the top dog here.

And another part of myself feared for my sanity and decency at the realisation of such sentiments. Idiot, I kept telling myself, by this stand of selection every whiteskinned cretin, Nazi, criminal is your fellow-aristocrat. I squirmed at the thought of that company. Besides, it demanded no effort at all. The worth of my degrees, I reflected, could be measured by the sum total of time and effort I invested in their acquisition. All my student years I mumbled dark contemptuous dismissals at honorary degrees and their holders. To be given privilege simply on account of my pale epidermis was, ultimately, an insult to me. It seemed to imply: the only excellence I can claim is the colour of my skin . . . nothing of the mind or soul or person. This somehow managed to stifle the glee of the unearnt accolade.

But perhaps most powerfully throbbing in me was the instinctive analogy between European Hitlerism and South African apartheid. I grew up in the shadow of German Nazism. At the age of fifteen, when the Germans occupied Hungary, I went into hiding with my family. For a year I stayed indoors, with the constant threat of apprehension and immediate execution all around us. All the anger and hatred of my youth was focused on Nazis and Nazism. We narrowly escaped discovery a couple of times: I saw their eyes and uniforms from close up, smelled the drink and madness on their breath. Evil and Nazism were made synonymous in the most personal and direct manner. While no expression could of course be given to this burning hatred at that time, it was very real and, in a strange way, pleasurable. To hate evil, wholeheartedly, with all one's being, somehow felt like fighting against it already, and thus gave one a profound joy, both sensual and spiritual. Here, in South Africa, racist tyranny suddenly disclosed itself as just another façade for the selfsame monster. This was not a reasoned conclusion, though of course one could—and had to—find full rational confirmation of the social and psychological and moral kinship between German Nazism and South African apartheid. It came with the force and spontaneity of an instinctive identification. What was done to blacks in southern Africa was, except for the plan of actual extermination, parallel to what Nazis did to Jews and gypsies in Europe. The motivation, the mood, the methods were similar : in fact, in many cases directly copied from the northern archetype. As if to revenge myself for my Jewish impotence during the '40s, I felt I had to atone by active participation in fighting the same evil there and then. A trembling impatience ran through me whenever an instance of remembered or directly witnessed wrong come to my notice, or when an opportunity of swinging a stick against the detested foe presented itself. It was this passionate personal involvement that underlay each one of the episodes that my own modestly significant tale comprises. In opposing apartheid, I was getting my own back on Hitler and Szalasi, the Hungarian Nazi leader. I was destroying a vile cheap temptation within my own soul . . . and fighting a good fight, good in its own right, in the context of African mid-twentieth century reality. Newcomer, outsider though I was, I had a duty as a human being, as an ethnic and religious Jew, as a rabbi, that is, teacher of prophetic Judaism and its moral implications. My personal vendetta—for it was that in a way —was only part of a much broader and, I believe, objectively warranted range of endeavour.

* * *

The first significant question that arises is: who resists . . . and why? How does the decision emerge in a person to pit his pitifully limited strength against a government, against a social structure as a whole?

The *why* and *how*, in this case, are inseparable from and depend entirely upon the *who*. Each person's background as well as his in-

31

dividuality determine whether he will accept the social situation happily or at least unmurmuringly, or whether, in some manner or another, he will express some protest against it. Some are quite literally brought up to be resisters. Others drift into it slowly. With some it is the upshot of an agonising reappraisal of attitudes and values. To some it comes like an act of conversion.

In Dennis Brutus' case the process was slow. Teacher, poet, international sportsman, he was shot by the South African police in the streets of Johannesburg in October 1963 and sentenced to eighteen months' imprisonment in January 1964. A man in his late thirties, married with seven children, a graduate in English and Psychology of Fort Hare College, risked his liberty and life in an attempt to breach the armour of racist tyranny by a clever levering of the Olympic standards of sportsmanship. Some years ago he was ousted from his job as teacher, later he was placed under the 'ban' which the Minister of the Interior is authorised to pronounce over any person, without either trial or appeal, to deprive him of any political or personal effectiveness in the country. Brutus is a man who was—educationally, economically, socially—as high in the non-white community as any. He had a great deal to lose. Yet he took a chance, and lost. Why and how did such a process take place in his development? One can only guess, but certain elements of the story seem open for legitimate conjecture. A highly sensitive man, the impact of injustice probably impinged on his consciousness very early. But passive resentment is a long way from active resistance. He may have started with schoolboy explosions, or harmless harangues at parties in woozy hours of night. There must have been the recurring temptation to accept, lie low, be silent, compromise, to make the best one can within the unfair existing framework rather than engage in the pretty hopeless effort to breach it or remould it entirely. For a man of great talent like him, alternative channels of draining frustration were always present. Like many others, he could drug himself with a sensual, hedonistic preoccupation. Or he could surrender himself to the protective wall of Bach, Gide, Saint Thomas and Paul Klee: fanatical aestheticism is some people's answer (black and white alike) to the raging ghastliness of social iniquity. Forms of mystical withdrawal, ranging from the crude to the subtle, abound in South Africa. You may smoke *dagga* or attend seances or become intoxicated with Saint John of the Cross; many do just that. Besides, in his own specific position, he was an enviable and highly respected man. The eight pounds or so a week that he earnt teaching made him seem immensely rich to most African or Cape Coloured wage earners or the teeming unemployed. He was known, quoted in the newspapers, unquestionably among the social and cultural *élite*—almost a white man, in fact. There was no social pressure from his own community to thrust him into a fighting posture; by and large, Cape Coloureds— or is it simply human nature in general?—prefer to wait for trouble to pass of itself, whether or not it shows indications of any such tendency. But gradually, the impetus of his own thinking, a systematic victory over many doubts and hesitations, drew him towards moderate, lawful and yet very brave action. A deliberateness and circumspection which often exasperated more impulsive friends characterised Brutus' resistance. He knew what he wanted, limited his endeavours to that single area, and set about achieving it. Until his escape, he did not break the tiniest technicalities of the suffocating South African body of law. Within it, but defying its mood and makers, he came close to tweaking the tail of racist fanaticism. And now he is paying the penalty whose eventual advent he never doubted.

Nevertheless, in the simplest, truest sense of the term, it was self-interest that impelled Brutus—and drives many others—to show opposition to apartheid. Dennis Brutus hopes, and with reason, that whenever he is freed from prison (and for that matter, his homeland as well) he will live as a truly free man. He will be allowed to vote and be elected to office, attain any position in society that his worth entitles him to. He wants to write and speak and publish as he pleases. He wants to be a citizen, wholly so, of the country of which he is native. And whatever chances of such realisation objectively await him, he wants such basic human rights and dignities to be granted to his own people. He wants his seven children to be educated for enlightenment, not for enslavement— and their lives to be fuller, happier than his own fathers' were. Brutus is fighting for himself and for his own. Even if he never lives to see the fulfilment of his dreams, they will have been natural, honourably selfish, elemental aspirations.

One might say that on the very opposite point of the spectrum precisely the same considerations occasionally apply. Take Bernard Johnson, for instance, He is an engineer, has a fine position, a pleasing house, wife, three children, two cars. But he knows that the position is untenable. With justification, he feels that he too belongs to South Africa. For generations the Johnsons have lived there.

And he realises that unless a peaceful and speedy transformation takes place, the white man's right and chance to survive in Southern Africa will be forfeited. Although he could emigrate, he does not want to. He loves his country, and has every right to do so. Despite the problems surrounding him, he wants his two sons and daughter to grow up and bring up children of their own there. For his own sake and for his offspring he resists what he understands to be a suicidal policy. There is nothing soft-headedly noble about his attitude. Primarily, he wants to maintain a place for the white man under the African sun. But he is aware that such a place can only be reserved—earnt—by helping, rather than trying to hinder, the forces which inexorably are shaping the pattern of tomorrow. In doing this, he arouses much hatred from his fellow whites. It is the presence of Johnsons which persuades the rising African leadership as well as their more and more courageous and numerous followers, that the struggle (in spite of all too tempting appearances) is not between white and black as such, but between oppressors and lovers of freedom, whatever their colour might be. If the white man is to be given any share in the future's South Africa at all, it will have been achieved by the rare Johnsons. Long-term, well-understood selfishness is the first motive for resistance, among white and non-white South Africans alike.

Next one must mention ideals, frankly, unashamedly. Dennis Brutus and, discounting his annoyed disclaimers, Johnson oppose apartheid because, beyond being dangerous and uncomfortable, it is simply evil. Even if no personal or long-term communal advantage would derive from the effort, one would have to participate in the struggle because it is one battlefield in the timeless war between right and wrong.

Moral, and more narrowly, religious convictions have a great deal to do with resistance in South Africa. The best-known names are undeniably those linked with the Church of England. Father Trevor Huddleston, The Reverend Michael Scott, Archbishops Ambrose Reeves and Joost de Blank spring to mind immediately. One must realise the primarily religious motivation of Alan Paton, author of the unforgettable 'Cry, the Beloved Country!' and of Chief Luthuli, winner of the Nobel Peace Prize. Perhaps it is a sad reflection that the clear spiritual lead of such men is not at all followed by either the laiety or the parish clergy. Yet the lead is there, a challenge to be taken up and, in itself, an act of heroism. Roman Catholic clerics have been less openly outspoken, but equally zealous in the parochial counteracting of racist theories. It is important to note that even in the Dutch Reform Church, long the official vehicle of segregationist ideas, high ranking theologians —Marais, Keet and others—have made fearless pronouncements and shown matching attitudes. In the Jewish community, this type of protest has been much more timid. The orthodox and reform Chief Rabbis of Johannesburg—Louis Rabinowitz and Moses Cyrus Weiler, respectively—have on occasion uttered mild condemnations of racism prior to their resignation: both now reside in Israel.

My own speeches and articles in this field were, I hope I am honest in believing, at least in part motivated by my Jewish identity. The whole ethical legacy of Bible and Talmud militate on the side of human equality and inter-relatedness; I consider it my rabbinic obligation to clarify this legacy and to advocate the concrete application of it in the social setting of the time and place. In addition, the historic experience of Jewish ethnic encounters became relevant to invoke in South Africa. Most South African Jews are second-generation citizens, children of refugees from persecution in Tzarist Russia. A notable segment came fleeing from Hitler's New Order in Europe in the '30s and '40s. I was shocked into vivid memories of the racial branding, ghetto building and deportation of my native Hungary during the Second World War when I witnessed the same techniques, based on similar sentiments, applied against non-white South Africans. Thus both the religious and the historic dimensions of being a Jew were active in whatever opposition a few of us manifested to South African Nationalist rule.

In due fairness it must be mentioned that adherents of certain secular ideologies showed as much dedication and self-transcendence as did certain leaders of religious creeds. Liberal humanists, democrats, Socialists and a tiny sprinkling of saloon-Communists into the bargain, participate in the resistance because they consider it a matter of decency and duty.

Perhaps a more psychologically astute observer would discern some pathological cases among the resisters. Hopeless, or heroic, causes do have a fascination for some poor, bruised minds and souls as well. One might pinpoint a few, perhaps, who find a channel for their aggression, for their personal need to vent anger and hatred, in the framework of resistance. But God knows it is easier and less dangerous in South Africa to hate the black than to hate racism: in the presence of other avenues of hostility, not many are likely to

D

fall into this trap. It is not impossible that a few masochists also have plunged into opposition; certainly, it is an effective way of asking for suffering. There are those who would rebel against *any* authority, just or oppressive. No movement—and South African resistance as such is not a movement, but a mood which involves several tentative movements and a great deal of vague individual attitudes and acts—is ever without a lunatic fringe. But it *is* a fringe. In South Africa, where the resistance in general (as far as one may today discern it, at any rate among whites) is a tiny phenomenon, the quota of unstable minds is negligible. On the whole, the opponents of apartheid are a sane and strong bunch.

*   *   *

If the motives that draw some men to resistance are numerous, the actual patterns of behaviour that they occasion are just as bewildering in their complexity. The spectrum runs from a frown of distaste to being hanged for blowing up a train. Again, the factors at play include character, social constellations and specific opportunity. There are those who find themselves irritated into an intermittent spasm of defiance, and those who methodically build their very lives into an instrument of demolishing oppression.

No worse mistake could be made than to dismiss 'mere' feeling and thinking as just that—mere feeling and thinking. From the unseen, unspoken bafflement at, dislike of, and, in time, recoil from, apartheid there develops by a logic of its own a policy of defiance. Amazement on reading a page about the French or American or sudden pain on witnessing an African maltreated, is often the seed of far-reaching action. True enough, a carefully nurtured pretence of guilt is a luxury all too often indulged. But a genuinely felt and pondered over insight or incident is what blossoms into intelligently coordinated, morally right, politically realistic conduct.

Resistance starts by seeing, knowing and caring. Strange though it may appear, one might say that more courage is needed in order to begin to see matters in their fulness, in order to open eyes, mind and heart, than to take the decision, once the seeing has begun, to act upon it. The fundamental reality in a situation like that of South Africa is a form of mental blindness. It can be both inbred or acquired. The ordinary white man simply does not see the black man before him. Either he does his utmost to avoid physical proximity or else he ignores what he could notice. He sees the black man as less than human, in what must be regarded as a moral and intellectual impairment of vision. Perhaps in order to remain sane in South Africa, or simply to remain in South Africa, such a device is necessary for a white person. The natural practice is to look aside, or look unseeingly, or force oneself not to look at all. It is almost unheard of for a white South African to drive through an African 'location' if he can help it. Neither shame nor fear keep him away. He will tell you earnestly that there is simply nothing to see there. How deep this unseeing goes is anybody's guess. But on the surface, it is a prevalent fact.

Thus, if a white man *begins to see* his revolt has in fact begun. For a white man born in South Africa such an acquisition of full sight is an aching and terrifying experience, full of bewilderment, danger and joy. It opens up unexpected vistas—and imposes an isolation and loneliness he has never known. Most white immigrants (indeed, all immigrants are white through strict Government selection) acclimatize themselves within three years. By some mechanism of the psyche they assume the partial blindness of the locals. Indeed, it is quite a fashion to place bets on how long this or that newcomer from England or Holland or Germany or the United States will moan with the usual teething troubles, belly-aching about Africans' rights and dignities. As a rule it soon passes. At first the tongue dries up, and shortly thereafter the soul too. One has made one's peace with South Africa: and in view of the fact that the material allurements and social pressures are many, such a transition is usually rapid and complete. But just as some native white South Africans—and according to the land's semantics there is a contradiction in this coupling of adjectives even—acquire sight, a proportion of the immigrants manage to maintain it whole and functioning. They are the source of most 'troublemaking'. Translating inner attitude into concrete behaviour is a natural, much less difficult if considerably more perilous step.

With some whites opposition exhausts itself in critical comments on official policy and prevalent mores exchanged at gracious social gatherings. A little risk is involved even in this humble rebellion; it rarely wins friends or influences people. Slightly more daring is protest that manifests itself in money. An anonymous contribution to the African National Congress (before it was outlawed) or to individuals victimised by the Nationalists did, after all, add some weight to the struggle. To pay one's servant more than the wretched going rate, say the equivalent of ten pounds instead of seven to a

37

cook per month, is distinctly unwise, almost treasonable. Some manage to salve a pang of conscience that way. Acts of small kindness and generosity to non-whites in personal contact, done in cautious privacy, may not contribute much to the radical transformation of the situation but still do a little, both to the recipient and the giver. Charitable and philanthropic work, so long as it does not openly or implicitly challenge white separateness and supremacy, is not taboo: a number of sensitive women, as also a man here and there, labour for Red Cross or Child Welfare, and in helping oil the wheels of a non-white hospital, nursery or school register their moral concern. Yet it is important to note that some extreme racists are willing to do the same thing. Just as one may be kindly though not egalitarian with animals, a nationalist may wish to see Africans better fed, healthier and more thoroughly drilled for useful if limited tasks, but sweep aside any notion of eventual equality as absurd or immoral. Welfare work thus may be, but need not be, the expression of liberal sentiment. Adolph Schauder, former Mayor of Port Elizabeth, did build a township, heartbreakingly drab in its actuality yet somewhat superior to most other alternatives in the land, and felt righteous in doing so, yet at a Bloemfontein convention of race ideologists thanked God with tears in his eyes for His wisdom in inspiring South Africa's leaders to seek salvation through the separation of the races.

Unambiguous and effective resistance begins when thought and sentiment find verbal, public expression. By the nature of the prevailing conditions, some subtlety is needed to make one's voice heard and understood, preferably without being too speedily muted. A man who stands up at a street corner and begins a denunciation of racism ends up within minutes in a police cell or a mental institution. On the other hand, too outspoken an assault on apartheid can be made into a treasonable offence. The danger in indulging it freely lies not only in the dire penalties law and illicit power make available, but in the liability that the voice is quickly and finally muffled.

In my own work it was these considerations which kept cropping up. Suppose Passover comes with its Jewish message of human freedom—political as well as metaphysical freedom—if I give a sermon on the topic, perhaps sixty people will attend, of whom one half will be soundly asleep, the other unable to see the relevance of general exhortations about liberty and dignity. It took me some time to find out that the most extreme racist may nod in approval while you praise human dignity, liberty and justice: to his conception of what these terms connote apartheid is in no way a curtailment. The African does get the justice due to him: a differential, second-level radius of rights. I learnt that either a naïve charity or plain dim-wittedness on the part of many listeners automatically drew the political fang from any broad ethical statement one may have cited. So the only resort that remained was ruthless, at times maybe childlike, explicitness. The moral of an analogy had to be completely drawn and hammered home tediously, shockingly, *beyond* the chance of unhearing or mishearing.

Immediately in the wake of the initial qualm about being heard and understood comes the next worry: what difference does it make if a handful of people do, at least techically, hear the words of say prophetic teachings as applicable to local and current conditions in Africa? A solid, protective phalanx of silence will be thrown up around any such disturbing squeak. Here and there a rumble will stir a local Jewish dinner party, 'Have you heard what that man said last Friday evening?' but after an outraged, baffled or at times consenting mumble or two, it will stop there, as if by a tacit agreement. We must protect him, and ourselves. Like family shame, it must never reach the curious, suspicious world outside. So I had to scratch my head to discover means of bringing the message—God knows, not of my own hatching, simply the plain text of Bible itself —to as wide an audience as I could possibly reach. At last I reached a somewhat obvious answer. Statements of religious leaders are often quoted in South African papers; in fact, an Americanised efficiency of press release and conferences has consciously and for long been utilised. I decided to make excerpts of my addresses on racially relevant topics available to the local newspaper. They pounced on what, in that setting, was exciting material all too keenly. National papers duly copied such controversial items. And it was at this juncture that hell broke loose in my tiny teapot. It was, to be precise, the refusal by the régime to grant a passport to a brilliant African student to honour a scholarship offered to him at a better American college that served as the first focus of conflict. Steven Ramasodi was one of Trevor Huddleston's discoveries; however, the Government spokesman delicately explained that it would not be in the boy's own best interests to be exposed to a value system which would upset his notions of normalcy. That week the traditional Torah portion read in synagogue related God's decree, forbidding Moses to cross the Jordan and enter the promised land.

I contrasted Moses' maturity and personal lapse from perfection with Steven's youth and innocence, except for his pigmentation. As I recall, I did not mince words about the judgment shown by a wise and compassionate God on the one hand and the verdict of pompous, arrogant, stupid little men on the other hand. My hearers winced while I spoke. Next day Port Elizabeth was agog with the tale; the *Herald* pushed copies under the doorstep of tens of thousands of homes. The following day I had phonecalls from Johannesburg, Cape Town and Durban. It astonished me how a totally unknown provincial cleric's peevish commentary could shake up people near and far.

From time to time, I repeated the experiment. In addition to sermons, spoken and printed, I contributed a few articles to local and overseas magazines. The Johannesburg *Forum* and the London *Synagogue Review* and later, Ronald Segal's splendid *Africa South* gave me space.

But in fact my own verbal or written expressions of dissent were a very minor instance of this type of resistance. One might mention Alan Paton, again, and Peter Abrahams and Nadine Gordimer and Doris Lessing and Harry Bloom whose novels entail a searing—at times direct, at times veiled—denunciation of racial terror in South Africa. Special honour is due to the few men of whom perhaps Jock Sutherland is the finest example. As Editor of the *Evening Post* he has for years skirted suppression while being the champion of literate and objective reportage and comment. By allusion, by biting satire, by cryptic understatement, yet now and again also by clear, courageous full description, he—and some like him—have upheld the tiny and diminishing flame of liberal, democratic appraisal of events.

A book ought to be, and one day surely will be, written about poor dead Christopher Gell. Son of a ranking English family, with a distinguished record, he joined the Colonial Office. For some years he served in India. There he was stricken with polio; his South African born wife brought him home to Port Elizabeth. Few believed that he would linger on for a decade. But he did, and during these years, confined to bed and intermittently to an iron lung, became the guru and inspiration of thousands of fearful white liberals and perplexed non-white discontents. He could not hold a pen beyond a few seconds; each word he uttered was a heroic effort; breathing itself was a crucifixion. But he wrote and he spoke. Apart from articles that were published in the most renowned political journals of England, Europe and America, he issued single-handed a periodical entitled, with sad appropriateness, *The Africa X-Ray Report*. In it, he described facts, both of South Africa and other segments of the emerging continent, that even an able-bodied reporter would have been hard put to unearth. His documentation was always impeccable. And the analysis and interpretation of data was devastaing in its accuracy and proven validity. Christopher Gell combined the trained historical-political perception of a student and past practitioner of international affairs with an indomitable daring. His own primary strength derived from his religious convictions. Christian and Hindu principles sustained his hope and vigour. Prayer and meditation were very real to him. The New Testament and Gandhi's writings were on the shelf facing his bed at all times. (The Mahatma, by the way, also cut his political teeth in the South Africa of an earlier decade: passive resistance as a modern means of globe-shaping was born on the Transvaal.) To Gell's bedside came, when Norah and the doctor permitted, humble little men in search of hope as well as visiting international figures and South African leaders of resistance. His tongue was at times biting; his mood often fiercely, infectiously gay. When he died, the Indian community was convinced that his next incarnation must be that of a god, literally. Many may have wondered when the London *Observer* devoted a distinguished profile to him—but to those who knew him, it was the merest gesture of respect.

In the strange, self-contradictory picture of South African society the white man assigns himself an oddly ambiguous position. On the one hand, the police state is becoming daily more stark and suffocating. White men's rights are diminished in much the same way as they were during Senator McCarthy's witch-hunting days in the United States of America. There is suspicion and restriction on everybody, white men included. Yet, precisely because of the flimsy façade of white superiority that both theory and practice appear to demand, patches of freedom persist, for the whites at any rate. A white foe of apartheid is heretic and traitor; yet, being white, he is still one of 'us', entitled to play the game on 'our' own terms. Thus a fair amount of white criticism of racial injustice can pass unpunished by law; social ostracism is sufficient retribution. Alan Paton may be prohibited from leaving the Republic, but he is not in jail. As long as the critic is white, and his assault on the régime limited to words, a measure of safety protects him still. The words must not be too inflammatory, nor should they be addressed to, or too readily attainable by, the non-white millions. Transgress these implied provisos, and you're in trouble.

To take the notion of equality and integration seriously enough to give practical expression to it is a very different, and much more severe business. Eyebrows leap at an anti-apartheid speech, but fists tighten till the knuckles bleach when a genuine social, or better still human, connection exists between a white and non-white person. In my own case, my talks and writings were deemed bad enough. The real storm began when I found the friendship of a few Indian, Cape Coloured and African men. It was not started with the deliberation of defiance. Neither love nor friendship can be acts of will. I encountered my non-white associates either by accident (at the home of white friends, or at a bus stop, giving a lift to a man waiting endlessly in the midsummer January heat) or in pursuit of concrete down-to-earth purposes, for instance, looking for a competent lecturer on Xhosa tribal religion or Hinduism for my Temple's adult study course. It was with a little surprise, but much delight and gratitude that I found intellectual and temperamental affinity, the very stuff of real friendship. I daresay we became friends, some three or four of us, neither because of nor in spite of our differing skins. Colour simply did not enter the question. Of course, as time went on, we did exchange views, experiences and insights on that matter too . . . but at no point was it a relevant factor in our human connection. However, our independently arrived-at convictions that apartheid must be opposed by all morally permissible means quite naturally made their reality felt in the course of our, for a while, shared lives. South African law, at that stage at any rate (in the middle of the late 50s) did not forbid personal and social contacts. No white South African in his right mind would dream to indulge such vices; no need to legislate against it, unlike against miscegenation. Without any special thought of popular opinion, my non-white friends and myself paid frequent and lengthy—and, may I add, delectable—visits to each others' homes. I must confess there was an element of deliberateness when, later, I would invite Dennis at the same time as I asked some of my unsuspecting white companions to sip coffee with us. To shake hands or not to shake, this seems to have been the profound predicament of my paleskinned friends. Some shook, some didn't, some simply set eyes on the darker guest, turned and fled forever. It was no secret that, to some of us, racial equality and integration were not only a theoretical perversion but a practice of depravity too. And this came close to being unforgivable.

Dennis and I went to Midnight Mass together at Christmas. We attended a recital by Pierre Fournier at the Feather Market Hall, and witnessed the Lunts at the City Hall, when my wife was indisposed to accompany me and the ticket was going begging. It was not yet against the law. The men at the door somehow didn't dare to interfere with the local rabbi, even when he was infringing an unwritten rule with unparalleled shamelessness. There were knowing nods, whispers, silences, cold stares and nervously averted gazes all around us. And when his vacation and mine came, we drove off to the North together: Victoria Falls, Zimbabwe ruins, Wankie Game Reserve—as lovely a trip as either of us had ever known. Yes, the sweetness of defiance both increased and marred its relaxed joy. My congregants stood quite aghast at such folly and immorality. When, at another time and in very different company, I toured the Transkei and, on returning, reported that I had spent one night sharing a bed with an African doctor, incredulity was total. They much preferred to think of me as a liar than as a complete pervert.

Examples could be multiplied, my own as well as other people's. Once we formed an interracial club in South End: suddenly the strangeness and the pathos of the land struck me with violence as I watched a contest. Amid the hoots and shrieks of amused brown and pink faces, two men—the white son of a former High Commissioner of South Africa and an African school principal— competed to see who could blow his balloon to bursting point sooner. How sad and silly and self-conscious did this attempt to bring human beings into human contact appear! Yet it fulfilled its goal, and was thus an instance of light in a hate-darkened country.

Looking back over almost ten years, many of my own attitudes and actions in South Africa strike me as perplexing. A lot of it I find rather juvenile. There was too much personal excitement, and at times, venom and self-righteousness in my speeches. At times I enjoyed the fight for the fight's own sake, revelling in my ability to infuriate sedate elders, and seeing society break into a storm at a mild remark or speedy gesture. Certainly, some people could have been won over to my side whom my hasty plunge into denuncia- tion only antagonised and pushed further away. Perhaps my demand for unconditional surrenders and refusal to compromise in even minor matters was simply childish, an arrogant proud playfulness to test my own power. I cannot, though, pretend to be unduly ashamed of it: only aware and, perhaps gently amused. My motives were mixed, my methods often lacking in diplomacy or realism or calm intelligent deliberateness, and the results frequently fell short of what I considered reasonable to expect. Or for that matter, from what I today—from my present perspective—consider to have been attainable. Had I minded my words more, and marshalled more patience to work out the logical implications of each step, probably much more could have been reached. If I am critical of my yesteryear self in this connection, it is not for having done or attempted too much but for having done too little . . . or lacking the maturity with which to make my endeavour much more fruitful. With some added personal stability, I could have transformed more of my community into committed fighters against racism. My command of actual facts —statistics, legislation, history, anthropology, Bantu and Afrikaans languages—could and should have been deeper. It would have enabled me to use the medium of magazines overseas for spreading what so desperately needed (and needs) to be brought to the knowledge of the free world at large. Maybe I should have published a book while I was in South Africa: the impact of someone present on the scene at the time of publication (even if that, naturally, would have to be in Britain or America) is vastly superior to even the most thoughtful retrospective summary of an exile. I might have defied the Expulsion Order which I was served and waited to be put into prison or else physically thrust across the border: surely a more dramatic posture than meekly skipping away at Government orders. Or much more demandingly still: perhaps I ought to have waited until I was naturalised as a citizen of South Africa, cutting all other national affiliations, and then throw in my lot with the organised opposition movement. But this latter alternative, most drastic of all, I often pondered at that time. I refused then to heed. It would have effectively silenced me for several years, and this prospect I neither enjoyed nor considered legitimate. And by the time I had my South African nationality, I might be too flaccid, comfortable, uncaring or scared to do anything any more. Even today I do not know whether this was right or mistaken.

On the organised level, very little white resistance is discernible at this point. The Liberal Party is devoted but too hopelessly tiny to really matter. The so-called Labour movement is well entrenched on the racist band-wagon; gone is the messianic zeal of the Garment Workers' Union of the pre-World War I years. White resistance, a symbolic pittance in some cases, is shiningly relevant in others; but it is confined to individuals acting as individuals. There is no white organised opposition to white supremacy . . . perhaps it is just as well, perhaps it would be a contradiction in terms. There is, however, a significant—if far from adequate—participation by a few white men and women in the overall opposition. Until its dissolution, the African National Congress (pledged to non-violence as well as to maintaining white rights, though not privileges, in a future free South Africa) included scores of white members. At successive Treason Trials, white faces—and Jewish names—were lined side by side with Indian and Bantu features and appellations. The newer, more militant Pan-African Congress—also suppressed—had whites other than Patrick Duncan among its supporters. While both organisations were of late outlawed, it is fairly natural to suppose that their scope and substance have only expanded underground. By conservative estimates, adherents of such subterranean manifestations must add up to millions. What is significant to note is that these movements have shown no trace of Communist inspiration or infiltration, have disavowed violence as a means of attaining their goals, and were never against white men as such, only against oppression. In the face of events like the Sharpeville massacre, this restraint seems most remarkable.

On the part of non-whites resistance—apart from the great if no longer visible movements—takes numerous forms. With many it goes no further than a disgusted expectoration at a beer hall *Gabfest*. But for multitudes, talking is a mere beginning, or viewed as a cheap substitute. There is, first of all, a new inner dignity. The black man may be forced to obey the white boss if he is to eat and keep out of jail. But the grovelling whine of servility is gone. Despite all discouragements, a cultural fermentation is seething among the non-white population. Books are read and discussed until the pages crumble from over use. The relevance of man's global experience and the speculative attainments of geniuses are avidly sought and applied. World affairs are currently dissected, and their local impact carefully sought. Will Johnson, the Texan, prove as zealous a civil rights advocate as Kennedy was? How does Galvao's U.N. testimony about Portuguese colonial holdings in Africa reflect on Pretoria? How soon can the Addis Abbaba accord of African leaders be expected to bear fruit? How does an Alabaman outburst of race hatred relate to terror in the Transvaal? The black driver, too, listens to the news while his employer cocks an ear to racing reports on Springbok Radio. As information spreads, concern, co-ordination, courage and hope gather momentum too.

There is, if not outright sabotage, at least the chance to go slow. The economy depends entirely on black labour. If it is literally illegal to stage a strike, one can decelerate the tempo quite maddeningly. Worse still, it can hammer home a clear and ominous warning.

No clearer example of such resistance can be found perhaps than the several bus boycotts in Johannesburg and elsewhere in the course of recent years. The Graou Areas Act—popularly known as the Ghetto Act—has uprooted scores of thousands of Africans and other non-whites from areas where they have long resided, for several generations in some cases. White industrial or residential expansion, speculative greed, ideological fanaticism or considerations of 'security' led up to these ruthless, forced transplantations. Men and women who would commute a distance of, say, twelve miles to and from a ten to twelve hour working day in the metropolitan region, were thrust another ten miles back into the bushveld. Another hour of crowded travelling time was added to an already exhausting timetable, as well as a couple of pennies in fares. It was this that brought about the boycott. Day after day, thousands of Africans walked up to twenty miles to work, and back, rather than board a bus. White opinion reached proportions of hysteria; police fingers twitched on the trigger nervously. Despite appeals, intimidations, arrests, brutal beatings-up and disappearances, the boycott held out long and unbroken. How human resources could measure up to the titanic demands of strength, remains a mystery. In the end, the fares were reduced, the boycott came to a conclusion. But in the process a formidable demonstration had occurred. The discipline and determination of African masses was brought home to local white public opinion as well as to the world's awareness. It was a portent of things that might—and surely will soon—come. Naturally, as far as white mentality in South Africa was concerned, one week later the boycott was duly forgotten.

Dennis Brutus' own specialised project represents a type of

46

resistance which is technically well within the framework of law (repressive though the law itself is in South Africa) and yet manages to challenge the very foundations on which such current legislation and the administration in general, rest. Sport plays an absurdly large part in the social life of the country. As if to channel pent-up aggressiveness and fears and to turn away people's gaze from the unsolacing face of reality, sporting events are the centre of much effort and attention. A test match overshadows almost any other occurrence in the world. South African participation in international sporting contests is a jealously cherished privilege. In a way, such events are felt to be a link with the world at large . . . a world which is growingly distant from, and justly hostile to, South Africa and what she represents. But the state Olympic standards forbid racial discrimination. Didn't Hitler himself witness American Negro athletes winning prizes from under the nose of blonde Aryan contestants in his own Berlin in the mid-thirties? Brutus, and a few friends of his, crystallised a consistent policy on that basis. If international sporting authorities are made aware of the exclusive, lily-white nature of South African sports, they must either instruct South Africa to integrate her teams or exclude them from the Olympics as unrepresentative. One way or the other, a blow will have been dealt not merely to sports but to segregationist society at large in the Union of South Africa. If their teams are excluded from the international arena, it will be another snub from the outside world and yet another proof of their growing, suffocating isolation. But if they decide to integrate the teams, a highly significant wedge will have been driven into the structure of apartheid. So Brutus and colleagues began their work on a shoestring. Interracial teams in many sports were established throughout the country. In fact these were mostly composed of coloured members, but theoretically they were non-racial, open to all applicants; in contrast to the official teams which usually by written proviso and in practice invariably were restricted to whites only. Then a campaign of letter writing commenced. The big names in Olympic sport, in Chicago and Zurich and elsewhere, were bombarded with appeals, fact sheets, memoranda. After an initial phase during which all this was waved aside as crank mail, success began to be noticeable. The *New York Times* and the *Manchester Guardian* carried stories; local groups in Britain, the United States, New Zealand and elsewhere took up the cudgels; demonstrations were held, letters to the Editor printed. At the Cardiff session of the Empire Games some embarrassment was caused to the South African official—and segregated—delegation. The preparatory meetings of the International Olympic Committee scheduled for Nairobi, then for Baden-Baden, in anticipation of the Tokyo Games, were forced to consider the question on the highest level. However furious the Government may have been, there was no legal handle with which to grasp this treasonable activity. And the very fact that Dennis Brutus' name was by then well known throughout the Republic and elsewhere, gave him a measure of immunity. The usual expedient applied against non-whites—sudden arrest and then disappearance forever—could not effectively be practised on Brutus.

By now, the project has grown to organised proportions. The South African Non-Racial Olympic Committee (SAN-ROC) has dozens of leaders and many thousands of affiliated followers. Beside the conscientiously pursued sporting objectives, the wider significance of this endeavour is hard to mistake.

At the United Nations in New York, Mrumba Kerina and Michael Scott continue a specialised, and magnificent, struggle against the South African régime, by focusing world attention on the terrible conditions in the territory of South-West Africa, mandated to the Union by a decision of the League of Nations. Non-white as well as white refugees from South Africa conduct a skilful and well-interrelated campaign for their beleaguered homeland from London, New York, Accra, Lagos, Trinidad. . . . Resistance does not stop at the border.

What deserves careful notice is the fact that absolutely no manifestation of a Mau-Mau mentality has occurred hitherto, or is likely ever to develop, in the Republic. One may discuss at length the morality and pragmatic results of terror as an instrument of political change: all too recent are the instances of Cyprus, Palestine, Viet-Nam, Cuba, Algeria. In South Africa, no such thing has taken place, despite abundant opportunity and provocation. No attempt on the life of even the most rabid racial hatemonger has been made: the one frustrated assassination plot was the work of a poor white lunatic. There is no basis whatever to suggest that recourse to that type of violence is in the offing. Not that it is altogether impossible.

Many observers are convinced that the ultimate, and no longer very far delayable, transformation of South Africa into a country that accepts its majority of people as full citizens, will happen through force. If that is so, by all evidence it will not have been

48

through the non-white population's choice. Liberty and opportunity they do desire, though leaders and rank-and-file have shown their distaste for violence. Only the future can tell whether there will be a last-moment yielding of the white *Herrenvolk* in the face of irresistible black demand, or else a bloody conflict. Alas, most pointers indicate the latter alternative. If so, the military challenge will come either from abroad—maybe from the free African nations, maybe from the big powers who might still wake up to the perils and wrongs of the present situation—or from within; more probably through a combination of both. Quite possibly preparations for such an eventuality are underway; one can only surmise their stage and extent today. But to say that coordinated military action might one day be invoked to free an enslaved land is very different from speaking of a sporadic, vindictive campaign of murder. The former may or may not be taking shape in secret places. Of the latter, however, there is no hint at all.

The motives and manifestations of resistance in South Africa are varied indeed. A scrutiny of its actual results should be illuminating. How does an attitude of inner and outer resistance modify thought, feeling and action in oneself, in the family, in the white and coloured segments of society at large?

* * *

The decision to show opposition, or the realization that one has in fact already shown resistance, brings in its wake a strange and mixed onrush of concomitant feelings and thoughts. Some of these may have been anticipated; others are a matter of shock and surprise. Personally, I found the first inner consequence of uttering public dissent to be an immense, almost dizzy elation. This happiness itself appeared to be the amalgam of several strands. There was, beyond doubt, an element of personal pride, an assurance of strength. That what a young twopenny provincial clergyman says might cause the opinion of a country to jolt, was shockingly—and pleasantly—new. Indeed, even before the open impact of such behaviour could assert itself, there was the delight of sheer defiance. It felt good, very good, to dare to oppose an entrenched government and the solid support of a whole social structure, the white segment at any rate. Quite possibly a measure of infantility was present in this emotion; be that as it may, the pure joy of it was enormous and lasted some time.

Added to the euphoria of being able to match one's individual

49

abilities against a vastly disproportionate adversary, there was the unmistakable awareness of the moral relevance of the resistance in question. Theoretically one may put up opposition to an ethically impeccable régime, and derive much satisfaction in so doing. Perhaps intoxication. But in the setting of South Africa in the mid-twentieth century, the moral validity—whether defined on grounds of secular morality or political foresight or religious ideals—of resisting the rulers appears to be crystal clear. And, though it may smack of Sunday school goody-goody-ism, it gives one an explosive sense of happiness to be able to do what is right and decent. To myself, coming from the mellow chiaroscuro of London life, with its subtle shadings of right and wrong in human affairs as gentle and elusive as is the English climate itself, the brilliant sun and stark blackness of South African outdoors as well as its ethical predicament proved most invigorating. At last, for the first time since Hitler's war in Europe, good and evil separated into their respective corners: the combat was unmistakable in its worth and implications. The refrain of the Negro spiritual, 'Which side are you on, boy, which side are you on?' slammed home here with the power of a physical blow. You simply had to take sides—trying to evade the decision in itself amounted to a decision of sorts, even if a feeble and cowardly one. To have accepted the challenge, made a choice—the only ethically honourable one—gave one a heady exhilaration. Yes, at times this may well have come close to self-righteousness, to the temptation to play saviour. But the fact remained that the resister did align himself with the forces of light against darkness in espousing the cause of black against white or rather the totality of the human spectrum as against exclusive white in the Republic. A crusading yet never fanatical dedication, buttressed by objective ethical norms, added to the purely human satisfactions of opposition. In various forms and degrees, these twin delights were shared by all opponents, white and non-white alike, of the apartheid régime. They appear to be inherent in political opposition as such.

And coupled with the joy, not in any way diminishing it and yet offsetting it and contrasting with it, there was a very real fear. Long forgotten terrors came alive in me as I found myself involved, in however modest a capacity, in opposing white supremacy and separatism in South Africa. During my decade in London, authority had ceased to seem menacing by definition. The policeman . . . well, he was the hackneyed Bobby of American tourist folders enticing one to Ye Olde Merrie England, someone to give patient directions towards an elusive landmark. Now, seeing a scowling Afrikaner policeman felt precisely as it did to slink by a Hungarian fascist arrowcrosser or a German SS. jackbooting on a Budapest pavement. Especially now that it was no longer only the African that was the target of the policeman's impatient, ignorant petulance but, potentially, myself as well. There is no denying that living a white man's life in South Africa can be and in many respects is a most enviable, easy existence. One does not work too hard; money is plentiful; social and scenic graces most generous. To risk the comforts, and exchange the, if temporary, life of relaxation for a threatened, possibly hunted style of being does tend to fill one with dread. Resisters, there as anywhere, had to learn to live with un-easiness in an environment of hostility and stark fear—current as they are in every phase of life under a tyranny—which focused on them by their own choosing much more acutely and ominously than on others. If you opposed apartheid, you could not but be aware that you were liable to pay for this indulgence. Liberty, limb and perhaps life too could all too easily be impaired. What was infinitely worse was the knowledge that not only oneself, but dependants could and would be victimised by the vindictive régime.

Thus there arose feelings of doubt and guilt from the mere, elemental fear. What risks am I incurring for my wife and children in actively resisting the régime? Have I a moral right to make my innocent dependants pay for my personal choice of aiding, albeit with questionable effectiveness, relative strangers? Am I doing whatever I am doing primarily to reap selfish emotional satisfaction? Or is my true motive one of sensationalism—what the public opinion of other countries, or of the black majority in South Africa, or an admiring posterity may appreciate? Am I simply out of my mind? Is this no more than a pathological exhibitionism clutching at an ethico-political rag to lend it a façade of respectability?

Far-fetched as these questions may seem, they were very real nonetheless. Brutus and Johnson and others had to face them; I certainly did. A quality of nightmare did intermittently loom large in the mind of all who in any way tried to resist. Part of it might have been ludicrous (though none the less vexing for that); the rest well warranted. The relatively simple pain of being scared for one's own future was compounded into a more sophisticated and searing torment by the recurring apprehension of hurting other, innocent people, and what, in 'Murder in the Cathedral', is dubbed the ultimate treason—of doing the right thing, for the wrong reason.

The consequence of the act of resistance within the resister himself is, naturally, the least open to objective scrutiny. Psychological skill can at best guess at true motives and real concomitants; introspective techniques are notoriously deceptive. But the outer, social consequences of resistance are comparatively simple to ascertain and describe. This, of course, only applies where the pattern of resistance is either deliberately or unwittingly visible. Theoretically a man may hatch a plot of sabotage and outwardly maintain a front of complete loyalty towards, maybe ardent support of, the existing order of things. Only where resistance takes the direction of open defiance, by word or action, does the immediate social response become discernible. Speaking from my own experience, this response shows a whole range of styles, as well as a progressive pattern of unfolding. When I first spoke out against apartheid, heated aguments burst out in many places. Many defended me. 'A young fellow, just cutting his teeth on the pulpit', some argued. 'What can you expect from a newcomer to this country? They are full of prejudice. But it will cure itself soon!' Others were less charitable—or is it more accurate?—in their evaluation of this scandalous conduct. There were accusations of ignorance, arrogance, recklessness, irresponsibility, immaturity. And quite a few people simply refused to notice anything—refused, that is, as a matter of deliberate policy. If nothing is said, it (or he) might just go away. But by and large, the initial reaction, apart from mild outrage, was an amused, jovial, though slightly nervous friendliness at this greenhorn's blunder. To Canon Collins, of Saint Paul's Cathedral in the City of London, no such generosity of first impact was extended: he was older; his word carried much more weight; and he came as a mere visitor . . . the best disqualification for any opinion. Tactfully, though rather clearly, it was suggested to me that the sooner my teething troubles were over, the better it would be for myself, and for them as well.

When it became apparent that my process of 'healing' was taking a long time, and showed no signs of acceleration, the attitudes and faces hardened around me. No longer was there the tolerant indulgence of the honeymoon period. When I had been there a year, 'He ought to know better by now', was the impatient cry of those who contended that two decades' experience was insufficient to understand the real nature of South African society. Within my congregation, fairly clear grouping began to appear. Some resorted to ostracism; others to bullying that ranged from gentle to crude. At council meetings resolutions were proposed and passed deploring, say, my vacation journey in non-white company. Informal little pressure-sessions were staged to impress upon me the folly, uselessness, downright immorality of publicly opposing official policy. In many voices there was genuine human concern for my own welfare, for Jewish survival . . . in others, a stiff, indignant anger. The mood of Jewish—and for that matter Christian—religious life in South Africa grants automatic tenure to a clergyman; thus my removal would have presented grave problems. Persuasion, or dissociation, semed the only avenues open to remedy the damage that I did. At first the effort ran along the former line. I was summoned, cornered, begged, bribed, threatened in turn. In due time, they attempted to bring pressure to bear through others. My wife was informed, in concerned whispers, what such stubbornness might lead to, and given hints as to how such attitudes should be handled. She behaved with magnificent loyalty under occasionally heavy fire. Then senior colleagues, serving important pulpits in other South African cities, were 'encouraged' to bring me to my senses. There were a few threats of resignation from my congregation; now and then a man got up and walked out ostentatiously from the sanctuary when my sermon took a supposedly tendentious turn. Confidentially I was told that the secret police had opened a file on me and that the authorities might revoke the Temple's license to sell liquor at social functions—a major blow to our shaky economics. The Sisterhood passed a resolution of its own to instruct me to 'cease and desist' in the future, as well as censure me for past infractions of decency. Nothing violent, nothing unduly large—but in their cumulative effect quite harrowing to endure.

However, (towards a questioning and critical white community at large) my congregants turned a protective shield· They explained away my actions. I was, they said, misquoted, misunderstood. The rumours about my interracial associations (though quite factual) were described as malicious fiction. They were partly protecting me, quite honestly for my own sake, in a spirit of kindness, partly watching over their own supposedly endangered security.

Later, when it was found that persuasion failed and pious deception gained little credence from outsiders and no co-operation from myself, the strategy became one of disavowal. The Board of Jewish Deputies and other organisations publicly stated that I spoke only for myself, not for Jews (which was alas true) nor for Judaism (which was a brazen lie). They added neatly that I had a right to express my personal views: and the Government to deal with its critics in whatever way they deemed fit.

Yet my congregation's disgust, anger, fears represented only one side of their attitude. As mentioned earlier, in the strange cliqueries of South Africa, even a wayward white remains white, and is judged by standards of his own tribe. Though I did threaten and denounce their accepted standards, I was a Jew among Jews, a white among whites. I was still among them, of them; a liability but also a moral responsibility. On the purely personal level, some of the individuals who were most fanatically opposed to the things I preached and tried to practise showed me real kindness, warmth, hospitality, consideration and friendship. Frankly, I found it hard to reciprocate: my own capacity to split facets of behaviour was less well developed. But I must state the almost embarrassing degree of human affection shown to me by some of the people I fought hardest against. In certain instances it may well have been an effort to bribe me (spiritually) into silence. In other cases, I must conclude that it was wholly genuine. My feud—for that is what it became, though not of my preference—with the congregation, with the Jewish community and with the white community in its entirety, maintained throughout the nature of a family quarrel. The prodigal son who ought to, and one day shall, return. The intensity of hatred had this internecine aspect. Not that it made it any the less violent, potentially at least. But in attempting to give a full and true evaluation, this must be included.

With small variations the reaction of the white community or its sub-set to me was similar to that shown to other known white persons who resisted. Ostracism, pressure, bribery, intimidation, as well as a pleading and hopelessly optimistic affection and tribal solidarity. Somehow the white South African cannot believe that when the chips are down even the most unnatural white would side with whom he takes to be his mortal enemies. As in Jewish theology, the gates of repentance are ever open. One lamb who returns to the forsaken fold of racism is worth a thousand meek bleaters who have never strayed.

A complementary trend also manifests itself in the white man's attitude towards white resistance. It is as though on one level of his consciousness even the practitioner of racism, or the abjectest conniver therewith, knew its untenable folly and evil nature, and nodded assent to resistance. A grudging, shameful sympathy not so much for the African victim of apartheid but for its rare white opponent, crops up in the most unexpected quarters. Not often verbalised but hard to deface entirely, a glint of admiration for resistance is at times to be found in the eye and heart of the very man whose practice is being opposed. Vestige of Christian or Jewish conscience? A throwback to standard of Europe and liberal-democratic traditions? Is it primarily respect for animal courage, or an implicit split-minded support of the cause it dares espouse? Is it guilt, Protestant Christianity's great and dubious gift to modern man? Whatever the answer this horn of the ambivalence butts through many an otherwise blank surface of white animosity to traitors. Once in a blue moon, a cautiously communicated message of identification gets through. A man may send you a cryptic note, or a book whose title or contents hint at his deep buried convictions, or he may summon up enough audacity to draw you aside and say, 'I am with you; it is right'. Though it happens infrequently, it does happen. People who for various reasons will not manifest resistance will indicate tacit support for those who do. Guilt, gratitude, affection come from strange corners in South Africa.

Within the immediate family resistance raises many problems. In some cases it is a family tradition, proudly shared and handed down. Parents and children, husband and wife, find a new bond of closeness in their united effort to combat an evil régime. The Gells' home was a tragic and surpassingly beautiful instance of this situation. In other cases, conflict occasionally results. Whether opposed on ideological grounds, or simply on consideration of expediency, spouses or parents and offspring at times are caught up in quite terrible perplexities. A young Afrikaner may become convinced of the vileness of racism, and be rejected by his wife, parents, even his own children, as a contemptible traitor in their group. Or else, a young Jewish university student, returning from a trip to Israel or Europe, imbued with ideals of human equality, comes up against his parents who do not care a hoot about ideals one way or another, but are terrified at the risks the young man's opposition might entail. And sometimes there are subtle nuances, as when a loyal young wife tries to suppress her fears at her husband's perilous activities, but her eyes give her away against her will, and he is torn between marital love and moral duty, or harsher still, one form of moral duty as against another, with no one to help sort out the puzzle.

Take, for example, the none too successful doctor whose wife takes an unpopular devoted interest in liberal causes. He might gently reprove her; or, in an irritated moment, his patience might snap and he may shout some biting criticism—a rift opens between husband and wife, one which touches on basic values and is thus hard to bridge afterwards. But maybe he will not say anything at all to her, either because he sympathises with and admires her work, or simply because he is tactful, or afraid, or simply in love. Still, she herself is aware that her activities somehow reflect on her husband's success or failure in society. If this leads to a renunciation of an expression of her own beliefs, a measure of blame against him and shame for herself is hard to eliminate. But if she persists, there will appear a sense of guilt and betrayal towards her husband, inasmuch as she makes him pay for her own involvement. Of course, such a schematic description is too bloodless to carry any of the all too real, flesh and blood, human complexities of the predicament.

A small shopkeeper of German Jewish origin occasionally indulges some sarcastic remarks about the régime and gets the reputation as a dangerous liberal—maybe communist, even! One day his son comes home from school with a swollen nose. His classmates chased him away from the game with a yell of 'Veetsak, kaffirboetie!' that is, 'Scram, you niggerlover!' The father is bewildered; it is unfair, victimising a youngster for the parent's supposed sins. But it happens. What should he do? Involve his son while still a young boy by engaging his loyalties on the side of the oppressed, thus making him feel alien and be treated as such among his fellows—or else let him grow up into a happy racist? As for the unfolding mind of the boy himself, he too is torn in different directions. He loves his father, but why does he occasion such painful social consequences? And is the old man's obsession with this African business a legitimate, admirable bit of realism, or else a foreign, shameful tag like his accent and eating habits? Then there is the mother who is anxious over her boy's safety but still, in her heart, knows what is right and wrong. And the younger brother sees and hears this with wide-eyed, half-comprehending wonder.

When I was taking a trip with some Cape Coloured friends towards the interior, among the numerous visits and telephone calls directed towards my wife and me, one stood our rather sharply: 'Did your husband at least get you a revolver?' My wife's instant response of laughter soon lost its gaiety. What exactly did this mean? The person who enquired was, we felt, a real friend. Was he out of his mind . . . or where we? She told me the message; I shrugged it off as silly nonsense. But somehow the tension it created persisted. There was a fair amount of gangsterism at work in South Africa, white and black alike. If something were to happen while I was away. . . . But even if nothing happened, the mere fact that I was willing to expose my family to that alleged risk prompted a reappraisal of our relationship. How can I do it to her? How can he do it to me? And to the baby? How dare she use emotional blackmail against me? An element of discord was inevitably created.

A very different battery of responses awaits the white resister from the non-white community's side. There is at first a great and cunning suspicion. For very good reasons the average black man does not trust the ordinary white man. He has no reason to believe or rather, he has reason not to believe in his veracity and benevolence. The white man who takes the first step towards opposition and is buffeted right and left by white disapproval at least secretly hopes — not for gratitude or appreciation — for some expression of fellow-feeling for his action. No such response will come, at the outset at any rate. Black opinion, if it notices one's gesture of defiance at all, is hard to mould. For one thing, how does the mild risk of, say, being expelled or banned (the white resisters' initial harvest) compare with the chance of instant torture or death that may be meted out to a black man for much less provocation, in fact for no provocation at all? Many Africans are, naturally, too involved in their own all too sorry affairs to notice a few white sympathiser's troubles. Some who notice, are not impressed. They suspect the motives and scorn the risks taken. They may be suspicious or jealous of a sly white attempt to disarm the growing resentment of the black population, or grab its leadership, or in any one way out of a thousand conjectured ways breach the spiritual defences (the only real ones) the African has. Of late there has been as much impatience with 'white liberals' in South African black contexts as in Southern Negro situations in the United States.

But this first reaction is most misleading. Because, after the understandable sniffing, testing period, there is bound to come and does come the realisation that (in the short run at least) the white resister stands to lose everything and gain nothing by resisting. And black leadership as well as popular feeling with all its hopes and energy and purpose, does need allies most desperately.

While some aloofness is bound to persist, more out of a sense of justified fear of white racist retaliation than from continued suspicion, the black community, in its guarded, shy way, does accept its white allies as equals: no more, no less than equals. Having tested and accepted them, the African masses surround the white resister with a spontaneity of joy, fellowship nad love that he had not believed humanly possible before. Not that a reward is needed, but in itself this tremendous spiritual and moral and human kinship, is the highest compensation a resisting man can ask for in today's South Africa. The wealth of deep laughter, the mingling of delirious daydreams with patient, realistic planning, and above all the natural intimacy of one human being with another in a just cause, is an unforgettable experience to anyone who has been privileged to encounter it once. In place of the first fearful suddenness of isolation, there rushes an assurance of immense support and identification. The white resister finds that in forfeiting the guilt-ridden, fear-studded, wobbly cohesion of the white community, he discovers, for the very first time, a feeling of real belonging to the country . . . a love of the twelve million as against the neurotic clannishness of the three, the fellowship of those joined in honourable aspiration as against the gang loyalty of oppressors. A fair exchange by any standard. As never before, he is treated on the basis of equality. He is not idolised, nor is he merely tolerated. He is simply a partner in a great, dangerous, most promising endeavour.

There is, too, the response to white resisters from the authorities themselves: police, municipality, civil service and, ultimately, the Nationalist Government itself. Towards troublesome foreigners, the simplest expedient is deportation. In case of prominent personalities (Archbishop Ambrose Reeves, for instance) this is gingerly applied, but applied all the same when all else seems to fail to bring them to their senses. Against citizens of the Republic, a gradation of pressures can be used. Primarily, there is plain intimidation. The very aura of the country is, by now, highly charged with fear. It is sufficient to hint at retribution without actually applying it, or even at times meaning to reach for it. To be taken at midnight or in the early dawn even for a mere questioning to police headquarters, can have salubrious results on the thinking of some half-determined discontents in the régime. And thereafter, official, legal and pseudo-legal means of breaking the rebellious spirit may be invoked. Apart from the 'ban'—which seems almost old fashioned next to the much more stringent measures of suppression—there is the provision of the ninety day arrest. Any person, on mere suspicion, may be detained for three months, without either a trial necessary to justify the action or an appeal possible to revoke it. On being set free after ninety days, he may immediately be arrested again, and so on, literally ad infinitum. Beyond that one can be dealt with in a variety of ways ranging from relatively minor indictments and corresponding punishments to the charge of treason, or even the advocacy of the change of a system of government which carries the death penalty. From petty harassment to execution, the régime has a full armoury to protect itself from those who would resist it. Thus far, successive trials (between 1956 and 1963) have failed to secure a conviction on either the sedition or the treason count. But every effort is being made, from stiffening the law to adulterating the judiciary, to make it stick one day soon.

When an African decides to put up resistance to the Government which rules over him neither by his choice nor in his best interests, a partially overlapping scale of consequences comes into play. Inwardly he will experience both the pleasure and pride on the one hand, and the fears and doubts and guilt on the other. Within the family, too, similar harmonies or conflicts may arise, Shall I endure the standard indignities and hardships of being a coloured man, or shall I add to my state the thousandfold risks of the proven rebel? May I endanger my dependants' livelihood and possibly lives as well, by showing opposition to what no man alone is likely to defeat? Are my motives true African communal loyalty or individual ambition or recklessness? There is little to differentiate the black resister's mental state from the white.

Socially, however, there is a world of difference. While in resisting apartheid the white man cuts himself clean off from the main body of white thought, feeling and life, and may or may not gain an African substitute-identification to offset isolation, the black man—naturally—only enhances his standing within his own segment. All his neighbours know that if he takes risks, it is for all their sakes that he does so. True enough, there may be a few dissentients. Some Africans will fear to associate themselves with a professed resister, for dread of dire consequences. A number of black men have decided to co-operate with the régime in exchange for a pittance of favours. After all, the Government can well afford to make it economically worth while for some less scrupulous Africans to sell a semblance of black support of apartheid. They will be loudest to denounce black disloyalty to the Government; the type is not unique in man's history. Yet, by and large, a black resister is accepted by his own community as the hero he truly is. And this social setting acts as a shelter for him too. Rarely does the black man's way of resisting oppression manifest itself in openly reported speechmaking or writing. From mouth to ear, from hand to hand, information is passed on, purposeful discontent. Few would allow enemies, be they white or coloured, to breach this protective blanket.

Now and again, a black man—this includes, of course, Indians and Cape Coloured as well as Africans—is brave enough to make his opposition public, known by the white community and its powers. A letter to the newspaper (published, if for no other reason, for its sensation-value even by far from liberal journals) or a personal contact not cautiously hidden, do arouse the notice and ire of white racist opinion. When Dennis and I went to a concert together, the ensuing questions were warranted: 'How can you do it to *him*, expose *him* to whatever consequences will follow? If they treat you, a white man, a public figure, charitably, what assurances do you have that the same patience will protect him as well? And by what right does he risk his wife and children?—and so forth. Almost instantly, retribution begins to clamp down on the non-white culprit. Public opinion brands him as a dangerous troublemaker, a Communist beyond doubt. From the undifferentiated mass of the loathed, dreaded 'them', one name is singled out as especially perilous and wicked, and the hunt is on. If the man, by chance, happens to be known (as Brutus was), the law unhappily must begin its own clumsy but growingly accommodating machinery. Things are much simpler when the non-white person is just another faceless Kaffir or Notnot. Police cells have witnessed countless beatings into submission or into the coffin; forced labour camps put disloyal energy to creative harnessing on farms or factories; the gallows yawns its greedy gap on many prison yards. Not counting a country physically and morally maimed as a whole, putting aside the sad legions of those crippled into dumb obedience, the number of those literally killed for their resistance runs into many thousands of non-white South Africans.

What more should one say about opposition in this, the world's most persistent and pernicious racial tyranny in this century? Maybe one ought to quote the ancient Hebrew Ethics of the

Fathers, 'In a place where there are no men, endeavour to be a man!'

Or perhaps one may conclude with a poem by Dennis Brutus who, like his country, is deeply wounded and cruelly imprisoned, but not yet broken in soul:

> We have no heroes and no wars
> only victims of a sickly state
> succumbing to the variegated sores
> that flower under lashing rains of hate.
>
> We have no battles and no fights
> for history to record with trite remark;
> only captives killed on eyeless nights
> and accidental dyings in the dark.
>
> Yet when the roll of those who died
> to free our land is called, without surprise
> these nameless unarmed ones will stand beside
> the warriors who secured the final prize.

GERMANY

Wolfgang Müller

1932 was a fateful year in German history. After several attempts to form a cabinet which was capable of governing had foundered, the President, Field Marshal von Hindenburg was forced to nominate Adolf Hitler as Chancellor and to ask him to form a new government. This was on January 30th 1933. At that time, this so-called seizure of power by Hitler and the Nazis did not strike me as alarming. On the contrary, I hoped in company with many others after years of political confusion, increasing internal dissatisfaction, street fighting between communists and Nazis, the enormous unemployment rate and the heavy burden of the Treaty of Versailles, that a strong government would arise which was capable of stabilising the situation. In the Weimar Republic after the First World War democracy had not won much recognition or respect. Its name was identified rather with defeat, poverty, worry and inflation. In my heart I was a supporter of the Hanoverian Monarchy, and I therefore rejoiced when on that 30th day of January 1933 the red, black and gold flag, symbol of the Republic, was hauled down and gave way to the red, white and black flag, symbol of Empire. In addition I hoped that the new government would expand the Reichswehr, which the Treaty of Versailles had limited to 100,000 men. For years the army had feared an attack from Poland and had therefore felt impelled to train troops illegally. I was one of those who spent several years between 1924 and 1934 giving unofficial military training to students and youth groups.

During my activity in the 'Black Reichswehr', as these illegally trained troops were called, I came into contact for the first time with the National Socialist defence organisations, the S.A. (*Sturmabteilung*) and S.S. (*Schutzstaffel*). The S.A. had originally been organised by Hitler for Party defence and propaganda and for street and beerhall fights. After 1933 it visibly developed into a vast body where, as a result of the co-ordination both monarchist and communist fighting groups found themselves inevitably enrolled. The S.A. leader Röhm was working to make the S.A. an independent group which would only lend the Party military support in times of crisis. Hitler drew the necessary implications from Röhm's attitude and formed a troop which would be loyal to him alone—the S.S. This belonged to the Party and was to consist only of the most reliable supporters. In June 1934 Röhm and many other high S.A. officials were murdered and the S.A. eliminated as an element of power. One month later Hitler rewarded the S.S. for its services over the murder of Röhm by making it an independent organisation placed under his own personal command. Without knowing it Hitler had done the Wehrmacht a great service in breaking the back of the S.A. Basically we Wehrmacht officers were favourably disposed to all military organisations; we even gave them temporary training. But the moment they shook themselves free of any state institution and became answerable only to themselves was the moment when they became dangerous. So in July 1934 I too was overcome by the uneasy feeling that the S.S. presented a future threat to the Wehrmacht. In those days I was still persuaded that the State rested on two foundations, the Party and the Wehrmacht, the latter being the only legitimate fighting force of the nation. Looking at it in retrospect I now know that the long drawn out struggle between S.S. and Wehrmacht, later to end so unhappily for the latter, was already beginning.

This particular autumn we had been testing a new infantry training procedure at an Infantry School near Berlin and were now holding courses for young officers. I was a Captain and in charge of the organisation of these courses. One day we received an order to take a group of S.S. leaders for training. 'Really a bit much!' said Major B, who as a strict Catholic was a bitter opponent of the openly anti-clerical S.S. I had put him in charge of the training and had great confidence in him as he was our best instructor. We decided to do a bit of probing into the S.S. Would my fears prove to be justified? We were met by boundless mistrust. For them we were the personification of dyed-in-the-wool reaction. It was thus extremely difficult to establish any personal contact with them. Not only did they distrust us, but they seemed to have a general suspicion of everybody, even their own room-mates, and throughout the course the atmosphere was cool and aloof. The S.S. leaders distinguished themselves by such enormous industry that it verged on the improper.

At the conclusion of the course the group was inspected by Obergruppenführer H. Everything we had vainly tried to elicit from them in conversation was now openly revealed by this officer. He praised the S.S. for their brave intervention at the time of the Röhm putsch and said the Führer had amply rewarded them for their loyalty. They now knew themselves to be the *élite* of the nation, the five per cent of the people called upon to rule. The remainder had to work and obey. He elaborated: 'It is for us to create a new modern state. Our examples are the great city states of Ancient Greece. We, the S.S., are the elect, the aristocrats, the creators of culture, so it is our duty to fight for our ideas and to keep them free of all defiling elements. We shall render harmless all political opponents who refuse to recognise our ideology.' One of my friends whispered, 'The man's off his head! How is he going to do this with his 3,000 men? The Wehrmacht won't just stand by watching and say nothing.' I nodded agreement. Meanwhile the Obergruppenführer continued his pronouncements upon S.S. principles, ideology and honour. 'You must deliberately set yourselves apart from all other groups. You are the new upper class of a pure master race.' This then was the explanation of their haughty and arrogant behaviour. They thought they were conducting themselves in an elegant and superior manner, while basically they were insecure and afraid of losing face. They felt their 'aristocratic' foundations were thin and sought to make this good by exaggerated display. But this only served to reveal all the more their humdrum, conceited and insipid characters. 'You are the nation's new nobility,' continued Obergruppenführer H complacently, 'and knowing this, your first duty is to make the idea reality and give it continuity by the procreation of children.' This new departure took us by surprise. 'I'—he was clearly proud of it—'have given my wife thirteen children. The Führer and our Germanic ideology demand of you that you too reproduce your noble blood.' He then turned to the first S.S. leader and asked, 'Are you married?'—'Yes.'—'How long?'—'Four years.'—'How many children?'—'One.'—'Why only one?' Embarrassed silence. The apparently disloyal S.S. man was then sternly lectured. So it went on; the next man was asked the same question. 'How many years have you been married?'—'Two'—'How many children?'—'Two.'—'Good, carry on like this and give the Führer lots of German children!' Thus we learnt that this was one of the chief duties of an S.S. leader and his rank was affected by the number of children he produced. I was still under the impression that the S.S., because of its small numbers, could not be a danger to the Wehrmacht!

Three years later, as a Company Commander, I was transferred to the small town of Tübingen. While here I was sent with other officers on an ideological course at the S.S. school in Bad Tölz. On the way I explained to my companions that we would have to be careful as the S.S. would be watching us and testing us ideologically. We would therefore have to be extremely wary in what we said and in our general behaviour so that they would have nothing to hold against us later on. One of the S.S. 'professors' there asked us our opinion of Charlemagne. As no one said anything he turned to me and asked what I thought. I stood up. 'The question in itself is unimportant,' I said. 'What matters is the opinion of the Führer. If the Party and the Führer determine that Charlemagne was a butcher of the Germans, we are of course with them. Charlemagne is to be considered the butcher of the Germans. But should Hitler and the Party be of the opinion that Charlemagne brought about the great work of European unity we will certainly allow ourselves to be convinced by them.' The 'professor' went very red and protested, 'But we are scientific people!' I repeated my viewpoint. It was only too plain to me that for the S.S. everything was a matter of propaganda. Exaggerated irony seemed the only way of shaking these ice-cold people. That evening we were invited to drinks at the Casino. We quickly arranged among ourselves to drink the S.S. leaders under the table in order to find out their real attitude to the Wehrmacht.

The alcohol loosened their tongues and all became clear: the longed-for aim of the S.S. under Himmler was to swallow up the Wehrmacht.

There was now no further doubt in my mind that both the Wehrmacht and Germany were gravely threatened. For my hopes that Hitlerism would be diluted and one day weaken were finally buried on that evening. But what could I do? Nobody in the High Command seriously believed in a danger from this quarter. To them the foundations of the Wehrmacht still seemed to stand fast without any sign of crumbling.

§

Not long after my arrival in Tübingen I began to get the reputation of being a Nazi. At first I couldn't begin to understand how this had happened. Only later, when the misunderstanding was cleared up, did I find out what had caused it. On my very first Sunday with my new Company I unwittingly brought upon myself the anger of some strictly Catholic officers by officially announcing that attendance at church parades would in future be voluntary. Until then the usual rule had been for the whole Company to attend church parade with the notable exception of the officers. I told the soldiers that I thought it quite wrong for anyone to be compelled to go to church, that I personally would be going to church and that anyone who wanted to should accompany me. As Nazi officers had made a similar rule everywhere it was presumably only natural that these Catholic officers should identify me as a Nazi. They were at first unable to realise that my action might spring from a totally different attitude.

Then came the pogrom night of 9-10 November 1938, later known as the 'Crystal Night'. Something had awakened me. I listened into the darkness. It must have been the extra loud watchwords and the dreadful insults to the Jews shouted in the streets. I got up and walked restlessly up and down the room. There was a violent knock at my door and in came my batman who announced in an agitated voice, 'Sorry to disturb you, sir, but the synagogue is on fire, Jewish shops are being destroyed and the local Jews are being bullied and taken away.' I went to the window and looked down into the street. Gangs of S.A. men and some civilians (including many youths) were running around, jumping onto lorries and shouting slogans such as 'Death to the Jews!' and 'Revenge for von Rath!' I remembered the seventeen-year-old Jewish boy who had murdered the German official von Rath in the Paris Embassy. How convenient this murder must have been for the Nazis. It gave them a perfect opportunity once again to call down curses on 'International Jewry' with its sinister designs for the destruction of Germany. But I knew their way of using political and historical events to suit their own propaganda. The memory of the conference at Bad Tölz was still very much with me. Furthermore I had the uncomfortable feeling that somehow the Nazis had a finger in this particular murder. The whole affair was just as mysterious as the Reichstag Fire in 1933 which a communist was accused of starting. This was then used as an excuse to ban the communist party and throw its members into prisons and concentration camps.

I looked out onto the street again and saw a boy who was picking up a stone to throw at the window of a nearby shop. Poor, misguided young people, egged on by years of refined propaganda to this boundless hatred. My batman came in with further news. He reported that Goebbels, the minister responsible for 'Enlightenment and Propaganda' had forbidden the fire services to intervene. It was therefore quite plain that this was a country-wide pogrom organised by the Nazis and not just an outbreak by the local S.A. They had often attacked the Jews before on a lesser scale, but tonight seemed to be the climax. Shouts and the sounds of wild brawls rang through the streets, the sky filled with clouds of smoke, flames leapt upwards. The synagogue burned. For me that night the mask of hypocrisy finally dropped.

How well had Hitler succeeded in convincing the country of his peaceful intentions! The truth was that the majority of the people were behind him. At home he had—admittedly by dictatorial methods—created order, done away with unemployment, and made Germany again respected. In foreign affairs he had achieved one success after another: the re-occupation of the Rhineland, the Anschluss with Austria and the incorporation of the Sudetenland into the Reich. Foreign powers recognised him as an equal— something that the Weimar politicians had never been able to achieve for all their efforts. And the nation rejoiced; as it always does when its rulers are successful. Under such circumstances any resistance must inevitably collapse.

And how the Nazis had lied with their propaganda. This night they were showing their real inhuman face. I told myself I must do something. The sky had turned red, a temple of God was burning. I must not stand by and watch this evil without lifting a hand! It looked as though nobody dared intervene. 'I might send my Company to put the fire out,' I said to myself, 'that would at least have a symbolic meaning: that the Reichswehr will not tolerate religious oppression and the burning of a house of God. But the point is, would this help the Jews themselves? A symbolic meaning—is this important enough to be worth risking imprisonment?' I thought of my wife, our ten-day-old daughter. For two days I stared at the burning sky and did nothing.

§

It was June 22nd 1941. We had marched into Russia and lay in the area of the Rokitno marshes. How were we going to defeat this country? I had been told by military experts of the enormous manpower the Russian army could muster. But Hitler and the Party were not interested in facts, they had been saying for years that the giant empire in the East was on the verge of collapse. No sensible soldier wanted this insane war. How we had hoped for an arranged peace with France and England after the Polish campaign! In April 1941 I had again become commanding officer of my old Tübingen regiment, having left it in 1939 to work on new infantry instructions at headquarters. After these two years I had predicted the Russian campaign. No one would believe me. When the time came I got hold of eight interpreters who were able to prepare my soldiers by telling them about the land and people of Russia.

We advanced into Russia and were south of Moscow in December 1941 when Hitler ordered a winter offensive. From the military point of view this was lunacy. Hundreds of my brave soldiers froze in this winter just as our ancestors had done in 1812. Without winter clothing, in thirty degrees of frost, we attacked over the snow without cover. Our weapons had frozen up. It was perfectly clear that this was the turning point of the war. I was particularly enraged by knowing that the S.S. were running about behind the front in thick furs while our people, who had to bear the brunt of the battle, froze. I sent a report about this to headquarters, but the more unpleasant the report the less Hitler would pay any attention to it. The German divisions melted away, the soldiers fought without reserves, without relief, and superhuman efforts were required of them. The everlasting night battles in the Russian winter were frightful.

In 1942 I became commanding officer of my own Goslar-Hanover regiment. Fairly soon I met an old friend who explained Hitler's strategy to me: the intention was to make up for lack of men and materials by the fighting spirit of 'Germanic man', by propaganda and miracle weapons. Hitler was intoxicated by bloodshed in the holding of untenable positions. And the German people only heard news after it had been filtered through the National Socialist propaganda machine. Of course I knew what Hitler understood by propaganda: 'Propaganda should not examine the truth objectively but should ceaselessly serve one's own ends.' The people at home could not see how they were being deceived.

I was anxious to maintain a good loyal corps of officers who were not blind followers of Hitler, so that the honour of the regiment would remain untarnished and so that I might rely on my officers in critical situations. Every time a new officer joined the regiment he underwent, without knowing it, a test of conscience. On the first evening I would invite him round for a drink and after he had-had a few drinks and was relaxed I would put the following question to him, 'Supposing I gave you the following order: "Our soldiers have been shot at from a village behind them. Go there with your troops, surround the village, burn it down and kill all the inhabitants including women and children." What would you do?' I usually got one of two answers. One was, 'Of course I should obey the order, I always obey orders.' The other was an indignant, 'I cannot obey such an order!' To an officer who gave the first answer I said nothing but merely remarked to the adjutant the next day, 'Lieutenant X is much too good for us.' There was such a demand for officers at the front that he would quickly disappear and join another regiment. If an officer gave the other reply I would take him aside and say, 'If you had carried out such an order I should have had you ignominiously expelled from our regiment.'

Meanwhile Hitler's leadership was doing everything possible to lose the war and drive the Russian people into the arms of Stalin. I had always emphasised to my regiment that excesses against the local population would only rebound on the army. We never had any trouble with partisans in the areas of Russia we crossed. We ourselves employed 200 Russian drivers who were well treated and therefore loyal.

During the Russian winter offensive Hitler gave a sudden order that villages be demolished so as to create a clear zone between us and the oncoming Russians. It was hoped to win time by destroying all shelter. But this had no effect at all on the Russians who kept on attacking even when the temperature dropped to forty degrees below freezing. This 'scorched earth' order was not only inhuman but quite senseless from the military point of view.

We were in a Russian village and had taken up quarters in an enormous farmhouse. Thanks to the cold I had developed such bad rheumatism that I could hardly move and had to be carried on a stretcher through the house and the village to the fighting positions. It was evening; I lay in a corner of the huge kitchen and quietly dozed. A few officers were standing by the stove trying to get warm. Suddenly a Lieutenant hurried in, bringing an order from headquarters. I ran my eye over the order and passed it to Lieutenant D. who was in charge of the rearguard. After a while he came up to me, stood to attention and said loudly and distinctly, 'I refuse to obey this order, Sir.' There was a hushed silence. Everyone knew perfectly well that death was the penalty for refusing to obey an order in war. I knew Lieutenant D. well— he was a clergyman and deeply religious; I valued him as an officer for he was brave and farsighted. The idiot, I thought, why couldn't he say that to me in private? Then, for the sake of saying something, I took him to task for being so noisy about it; why couldn't he make his point without shouting? This only made him more determined. 'I'm sorry, sir, but this order goes against my conscience. I can't take it upon myself to drive women, children and old men out of their houses into the freezing cold and then burn their village.' I was struck by the thought that the Lieutenant was intent on becoming a martyr. 'Give me the order,' I said, and read out: 'As soon as the village has been cleared the rearguard is to set light to it.' Of course this order must not be carried out— but Lieutenant D. had put me in a difficult position. If I were now to say that the order was to be disobeyed, the morale of the troops would be affected. Then I had a brainwave. 'As you wish, Dietrich,' I said, 'I relieve you of your command. Send me your Sergeant Major, he will take over.' When he had left the room, in which the others were still sitting openmouthed, I said in a loud voice, 'I order you to forget this incident at once.' I then had myself carried into my room to await the Sergeant Major. It was obvious that this order had to be handled with duplicity; it would have to be carried out and yet at the same time not carried out. Sergeant Major F, an experienced and canny old soldier, was just the man for this. So when he came in I said, 'Of course this order from

Division has to be carried out, but I'm sure you realise that your men's lives are more important than the burning of a village. You've been fighting the Russians for quite a time now and know as well as I do that they're after you as soon as they see flames.' He understood my meaning at once. 'I might mention,' I continued, 'that there are some bundles of straw lying in front of the village—you can burn those.'

This senseless order of Hitler's was carried out to a greater or lesser degree all along the front until our commander, General Hossbach, countermanded it in no uncertain terms—an action which incurred Hitler's deepest displeasure.

A few days after Hossbach's order I was in my billet getting ready to move off when all of a sudden I saw smoke coming under the door. I hobbled painfully down the stairs and was overcome by a dreadul fit of coughing when I got outside the door. Then I saw that a fellow from another troop was setting fire to the neighbouring house. I yelled at him to stop at once, but he just grinned impudently and carried on. Again I threatened him without success, so I told my batman to fetch a whip, lashed him with it and put him under arrest. It was impossible to let such insolence and lust for murder go unpunished. Thanks to this incident our retreat did not go unnoticed; the Russians shot at us wildly from behind and we lost four dead and seven wounded. General Hossbach approved of my action and ordered severe punishment for such firebugs.

§

At the end of September, after the 'Citadel' offensive, I stood before the sad remains of my regiment to take farewell. Out of 1400 men there were 75 left, of the 70 officers 35 were dead and 33 wounded. My rheumatism had crippled me to such an extent that I had to give up command of my regiment and be transferred to a hospital in the Sudetenland.

For hours on end I lay in my bed and reflected with growing disquiet: militarily Germany had lost the war. My thoughts revolved round the one question: how can Germany be saved? I reached for a book that was on hand wherever you went in the services and read: 'State authority cannot be an end in itself, for if it were, any tyranny in the world would be unassailable and sanctified. If the government in power is clearly leading a people to destruction, rebellion becomes not only a right but a duty.' Just as I had reached this bit S.S. Sturmbannführer L. came through the room. I called him over and read out the passage in question. His face went very red and he roared, 'Who wrote that? The man should be in a concentration camp!' Astonished I replied, 'Who?—Adolf Hitler!'

I was always finding that many Nazis, even those in high positions, had never read *Mein Kampf*, Hitler's only book.

In early 1944 I went to Hitler's headquarters in Rastenburg, East Prussia, to resume my old job of compiling infantry instructions. All the most secret infantry reports from the front went through my office and I had a full picture of the ghastly situation: Germany was in a bad, indeed hopeless way. As far as manpower and materials were concerned the army's state was catastrophic. Why did the Supreme Command entirely fail to take this into account? Could we, if it came to the point, even defend our own borders? We on our staff knew the answer to be negative.

My office was only seven kilometres away from Hitler's Bunker. Not once did I catch a glimpse of him in all the time I spent there, and indeed only a very small circle of people were permitted to see and speak to him. It was years now since he had shown himself to the public and he lived in impenetrable isolation. A threefold barrier surrounded his headquarters, known as the 'Wolf's Lair'.

To get into the centre of his headquarters from Rastenburg you had to pass through seventeen security checks. The Führer's S.S. guard watched over the 'greatest war leader of all time' with amazing care and great mistrust towards all visitors, so that it was impossible to pass through the barriers if armed. Hitler was a vegetarian; he had his food prepared in his own kitchen and tasted beforehand by his personal doctor.

Now and then details of Hitler's conversations percolated through the barbed wire fences and minefields that surrounded the 'Wolf's Lair' (security measures had cost a total of twenty eight million marks). A General remarked that Hitler had said, 'Don't go supposing that the Western Powers will make a separate peace with me. No one will do that.' The war was lost—not only militarily but politically also—of that I was sure. With this my last secret hope was shattered. I remembered another utterance confided in me by the same General. A leading officer had referred to the catastrophic situation on the Eastern Front and was talking of unrest among the people when Hitler shouted, 'If the German people won't understand me and won't fight, then it must perish!'

The Supreme Command became disgruntled by my perpetual

73

warnings and reports which painted the situation at the front in its true colours, and I was therefore transferred on July 9th 1944 to the High Command of the Reserve Army in Berlin. I was in command of the infantry, which was stationed outside Berlin in the former Olympic village of Döberitz. The infantry school had long been here and, in addition to my normal duties, I was given authority over the training at this school; but I had no disciplinary authority. The commanding officer was General Hitzfeld.

On July 11th I had to go and see my superior General Olbricht and his Chief of Staff Colonel Merz von Quirnheim. I drove slowly through Berlin to the Bendlerstrasse in a grey open car. My thoughts were far away in Hohensalza with my wife who was expecting her fourth child at any moment. I was worried about her health and had tried to telephone her several times during the morning. I could sense a tense atmosphere in Berlin. Lost in thought I went up the broad staircase. At this moment I thought of an order which Colonel S., one of my officers, had mentioned to me. Hitler had commanded that German partisans be armed with weapons which were no longer of any use to the troops at the front. I was furious that people should be armed with useless weapons and thus be sacrificed in cold blood, and made no secret of it. Whereupon Colonel S. signified with a wink that these weapons did not exist.

Now again I felt anger mounting in me and considered myself in duty bound to emphasise to General Olbricht the disastrous state of the infantry and Hitler's madness in allowing the people to bleed to death. Things couldn't go on like this, something had to happen.

I stood before Olbricht and gave him my usual résumé . . . '500,000 dead in the infantry alone . . . no replacements . . . no equipment . . . the situation worsening every day . . . the only possible decision is to make peace . . . what the Supreme Command is now ordering I cannot reconcile with my conscience.' Olbricht agreed with me and said that something decisive would soon occur. He parted from me with the words: 'Our views will prevail, Colonel. In the future we will have to work together closely to achieve our aim.' Going through the ante-room I met Olbricht's chief of staff Merz von Quirnheim and once again stated my opinions. He agreed with me completely and said that the war was already hopelessly lost however many strokes of good luck we might have. The Eastern Front was on the point of collapse,

74

the Western Powers had succeeded in landing in Normandy, and we could no longer hope for any real support from our allies. Hitler's hope that the enemy coalition would break up was completely absurd. He shook his head, 'An alliance of even the most contrary forces won't go and collapse just before the moment of victory over a common foe. In any case we must regard the situation in Germany itself with a pretty sober eye. The armaments industry is visibly shrinking, fuel supplies are being exhausted, and as a result the German armies will very soon be crippled. In view of all this Hitler is in duty bound to make peace.' I replied that I had heard at Headquarters that under no circumstances would Hitler agree to a peace treaty. For a while we were silent. 'So all we can do is draw the necessary conclusions,' I heard Merz say decisively. 'We owe it to the nation and our own consciences to take action. You can be quite sure that our opinion is shared by most people here at the War Ministry. Something will happen. We need your support just as we need the courage and strength of many other like-minded people.'

Exactly what plot was being hatched in the Bendlerstrasse I couldn't quite make out, but it was not my job to investigate. I told myself that in a Police State like Hitler's a *coup* could only be successful if the inner circle of conspirators was kept as small as possible. I resolved to hold myself in readiness and to win over my own troops. Back in my office I found a telegram: 'It's a boy. Mother and baby doing well.' At least one ray of light!

On July 15th a trusted colleague of General Olbricht informed me that the officers in the Bendlerstrasse were ready to strike. He carefully hinted that matters might even be brought to a head that very day. I was ready.

So the decision was made! Was this high treason? In the first moments I was worried by this thought; but could I really recognise Hitler and his S.S. as a legal authority? Or must I not rather do something at the very first opportunity to attack the régime? I tried to imagine how the rebellion would go. Would it succeed? I reckoned on ten per cent chance of success. For resistance is an enormous risk in any state that bases its strength on an army of spies.

The day passed uneventfully. I asked the Bendlerstrasse for two days leave. When I drove through Berlin at about five p.m. all troops were standing at emergency stations. It surprised me that I had been granted leave. Was anything going to happen?

Immediately after my return on July 17th I confided in my

closest colleague Major Ludwig and my batman Heinrich Weber. I had got to know them both thoroughly during the two years on the Russian front and was sure I could trust them. Heinrich came from the Sudetenland and was a Social Democrat. 'We're going to rise against Hitler,' I told him. He replied, 'Then I'm all for it, sir. We can't allow ourselves to be oppressed forever! The way Hitler's treating the Czechs is quite wrong, and so is the attack on our Catholic Church.'

I was pleased with his reaction and told him to get the weapons ready. I then tried to talk to my officers about the revolt. It was not nearly as hard as I had expected to convince them of the need to act against Hitler. For year after year they had been compelled to collaborate with the Nazi Party and had grown to loathe its authority. I could count on them without a doubt.

On July 19th I went to inspect the anti-aircraft school at Altwarp. The next day, July 20th, I arrived at the Stettin Station in Berlin. My grey jeep was waiting outside the station. The driver opened the door and excitedly announced, 'Sir, there's been a radio report from the Führer's headquarters that someone's tried to blow the Führer up!' I got into the car at once and had myself driven to Döberitz by the quickest possible route. As we went along my driver continued: 'Several of the people standing near Hitler were killed or wounded. The Führer is alive and only slightly hurt.' My companion, Lieutenant Goedeke, asked me whether there was any sense in carrying on with the revolt if Hitler had escaped. I replied, 'The rebellion will be in full swing now. We can't dream of leaving the Bendlerstrasse conspirators in the lurch. In any case the announcement that Hitler is still alive could easily be a deliberate lie on the part of the S.S. We raced through the centre of Berlin at breakneck speed, weaving in and out of endless Panzer columns driving towards the government quarter. So the revolt was on. I spoke loudly to make my voice heard above the noise, 'We must save what can be saved. We can't let our families be ruined and destroyed. Our aim is to make peace. Therefore Hitler and the S.S. are our enemies!' We raced into Döberitz. All around us the troops were at emergency stations. It was eight p.m. Captain K. ran out to greet me in an agitated state. 'It's a good thing you've come, Colonel. General Hitzfeld is away at a funeral. The O.K.H. warned us for action hours ago but we are going to have to wait because the Colonels can't agree on the next step. Colonel, you must do something!'

Hurrying up the steps I swiftly reflected that, although without real authority, I must stake everything on one throw. I flung open the door and shouted, 'The Infantry School will obey my commands!' Everyone was immediately silent. The tense atmosphere among them struck me most forcibly. Then they all began talking wildly again without being able to decide on any solution. Colonel L., whom I knew to be a Nazi, came up to me and questioned whether I had the right to issue orders. I overruled him, but unfortunately he was quite correct. Others demanded action after all this waiting about. Those loyal to Hitler entered the debate, saying that we ought to wait, seeing that the situation was so confused. I asked for silence and had the order brought to me. It was from the Chief of Staff of the Reserve Army Colonel Claus Count Schenk von Stauffenberg and ran as follows: 'The Führer is dead.' I stopped for a moment, for someone had crossed out this sentence. 'A clique led by Himmler and Keitel is trying to seize power. In order to save the German people from destruction the army is taking over executive power. The Waffen S.S will at once be amalgamated into the army and this is to be presented to the troops of the Waffen SS as a *fait accompli*. All resistance is to be broken ruthlessly. The Döberitz Infantry School is to occupy (1) the radio stations in and around Berlin, (2) Oranienburg concentration camps 1 and 2.' So Stauffenberg had invented an S.S. putsch in order to get the troops on his side by feigning legality.

I interrupted the continuous chattering and loudly announced, 'This order will of course be obeyed!' 'Yes!' some of them cried, 'Orders are orders!' But others shouted, 'We won't march under any circumstances! There's certainly a military putsch behind this order.'

Lieutenant Goedeke called me into a corner and whispered, 'The battalion commanders are itching to get going. They think that any more delay will give the S.S. time to collect their forces and that the result will be unnecessary bloodshed.' I asked him whether the troops were ready to march off. 'Yes! Only the training battalion is out on night exercises. So the Oranienburg concentration camps can be taken in a couple of hours.'

I decided to speak to the troops. On the way I wondered whether it would be right to declare openly and honestly that we wanted to overthrow Hitler without giving any formally legal justification for our intervention. No. By far the best course was to act as though

77

what we were doing was completely lawful. The soldiers must not be made to run any risk in the case of failure. I appeared before the troops and said, 'Hitler is dead. He has nominated Goering as his legal successor. The S.S., under Himmler's leadership, has overthrown Goering and illegally seized power.' The soldiers, mostly veterans of the front, stared at me in silence. I knew their wishes and their longing for peace at last, so I continued: 'Goering wanted to make a separate peace with England and the U.S.A., but now that the S.S. is in power a separate peace is impossible. No one will make peace with the S.S. Our people, our families and we soldiers who have risked our lives on all fronts, we want peace. Therefore let us now fight for the legal government!' The troops shouted enthusiastic agreement and the battalion commanders gave the word to march off.

I returned to my headquarters. The essential was achieved: the troops were marching. I sensed the danger that the officers who were still hesitating might take it into their heads to call the troops back because of my lack of authority. I would have to forestall them. So I telephoned General Hitzfeld, briefly described the situation at the School and repeated Stauffenberg's orders. Whereupon Hitzfeld ordered me to proceed unhesitatingly against the S.S.

Colonel L. greeted me with the reproach that I was acting too harshly towards the S.S. I could see that I was not succeeding in reassuring the officers, let alone in winning them over. So I decided to drive to the Bendlerstrasse in order to obtain official authority from my superior officer, General Olbricht.

Once again I was accompanied by Lieutenant Goedeke. With the onset of darkness the Berlin streets had undergone a ghostly change. Nowhere were armoured cars, infantry or sentries to be seen. The people of the city had anxiously withdrawn into their houses.

We arrived at the Bendlerstrasse. I was thunderstruck; even here at the central point of the conspiracy not a sentry was to be seen. I ran up the stairs and through several corridors, noting with some satisfaction that a group of arrested S.S. leaders was standing around in a corner; on the third floor I saw General Olbricht, downcast and with a gloomy face, entering his office. The same atmosphere reigned in his ante-room, which I now entered. His secretary nodded to me sadly. It was plain that the outlook for the conspirators now looked black. To break the oppressive silence I asked if anything new was happening. She shook her head. I was just leaving the room when I bumped into Merz von Quirnheim.

I formally reported: 'Infantry School occupying radio stations. I have carried out your orders with difficulty. The training battalion is on night exercises and will be back in a few hours. I request full powers.'

Merz asked, 'Where is General Hitzfeld?'—'In Baden. At a funeral.'—'Pity. Yes . . . what are we going to do now?'—'I suggest we send the training battalion here so that at least you have one proper troop to protect you.'—'Agreed!'—'Would you please give me that in writing,' I said, 'otherwise the officers at the Infantry School will refuse to obey.'—'Yes, you'll get unconditional authority. Bring the training battalion here. We need you personally.'

He dictated the order to his secretary, then went into Olbricht's office to have it signed. With the order in my hand I left Merz von Quirnheim. In the doorway I was overcome by a dark premonition that he would soon have to die for the salvation of Germany. I had often had the same feeling in dangerous situations at the front when I had spoken with soldiers shortly before their death. I turned and went back to Merz von Quirnheim to give him my hand. We looked each other steadfastly in the eye as an unspoken promise.

We left the building at 9.45 p.m. As we crossed the courtyard troops were marching in. 'Good, at least there are some troops here now,' I said to Goedeke without guessing for a moment that this was the firing squad coming for Olbricht, Merz von Quirnheim, Count Stauffenberg and his adjutant von Haeften.

I urged my driver back to Döberitz at headlong speed. Every minute was valuable. Could the situation still be saved? Was Hitler really alive or was this merely a refined piece of deception on the part of the S.S.? I looked at my watch: 11 p.m. With the order in my hand I entered the School Headquarters. Colonel L. hurried up to me: 'The attempted revolt has completely collapsed. Hitler is alive,' he gloated triumphantly. 'We have just heard from the Bendlerstrasse that the leading conspirators have been shot. So it wasn't as you said an S.S. putsch,' he continued sarcastically, 'but a military uprising led by Generals Beck, Olbricht, Hoeppner and Field Marshall von Witzleben. Count Stauffenberg's assassination attempt was, thank goodness, a failure. Goebbels has personally confirmed this to me.' The officers looked at me in silence. 'Well, why doesn't one of you 150 per cent Nazis put me under arrest?' I thought. 'But, of course, not one of you dares risk anything before the situation is quite clarified.'

Without a word I turned on my heel and went off to my office. The officers in my detachment had heard of the changed situation and were waiting for me. What was to be done? We were of course agreed that the troops and as many as possible of the officers must be protected. We were now all in the same dangerous position and I therefore declared, 'We must try to cover ourselves and to disguise our motives; we have got to deceive the Gestapo. I suggest we say that we had no idea that it was Stauffenberg who tried to assassinate Hitler; we had simply been told that Hitler was dead and that the S.S. was illegally trying to seize power. We must say that we supposed there to be a struggle inside the Nazi Party and that Himmler, leader of the S.S., had overthrown Goering the legitimate successor; that is the only way we can justify the intervention of the troops.' They agreed with me and we shook hands with a promise to stick together in the dangerous times ahead.

I left Döberitz to go to Berlin and find out how the land lay. On the way Major R. stopped my car and told me that there were no more Generals left in Berlin. The City Commandant von Hase had just been arrested. So I took over temporary command of the troops in and around Berlin, and drove to the Ministry of Propaganda. S.S. Obergruppenführer Jüttner, a fanatical ice-cold type, welcomed me with the information that the Führer had placed the home army under Himmler's command. This then was the end of the Reichswehr. I left the Ministry in a hurry—there could now be only one decision. Any attack on Hitler without the Bendlerstrasse leadership was pointless.

Back in my office I received a signal which informed all conspirators throughout the Reich that the attempted uprising in Berlin had been completely crushed. By now it was three a.m.

The following morning all commanders were informed that they 'would today have the opportunity of hearing the greatest man of the millenium speak.' This must be Himmler. I had myself driven to the Bendlerstrasse for the speech. When I arrived Himmler had already begun. I walked up and down the corridor. Now the events of the past twenty hours came before me in all their significance and I was thoroughly depressed. Through the door I could hear Himmler's didactic voice. The air was filled with worn out propaganda slogans: 'Greater German Reich . . . miracle weapons . . . the conquest of the East . . . no retreat . . .' So Himmler wanted no retreat, no peace, simply to sacrifice in cold blood the whole German people, including women, children and the old. I stood still by the door through which his monotonous voice continued: 'Germans do not surrender. We will defend ourselves to the last drop of our noble blood! We will not give up one inch of our sacred German soil to the enemy.' I felt for my pistol in my trouser pocket. 'The unscrupulous swine,' I thought, 'I'll kill him! At any moment he'll leave the room.' But he carried on, talking of 'German honour', 'the noble race', 'true pride' and 'the historic mission of a master race'.

I stood there uneasily and asked myself, 'What is the purpose of this deed? The greatest murderer in Germany would be executed not by the victorious Allies but by a German. So we Germans would show that we are not all blind followers of this system and that we do not all silently and helplessly put up with Hitler as our irrevocable fate. I'll kill him,' I repeated and grasped my pistol tightly. 'What will be the consequences?' Quickly and with misgivings I realised the answer. Inside the room the officers were applauding Himmler's speech. He would come out any minute. But I was wrong. His voice was booming again. He was depicting the barbaric punishments in store for the rebellious officers. Again I was sunk in thought, remembering the assassination of Heydrich. When that took place the S.S. had deliberately liquidated a whole village which had had nothing whatever to do with the affair, simply in order to cow people. And the results of my action? I saw my wife and four children, my mother and my brothers and sisters. Send them all to their deaths? But surely this deed had to be done? I stood there irresolutely. Himmler was responsible for the countless Jews murdered in concentration camps; again I seemed to hear those words of his which someone had once repeated to me: 'The only thing that interests me about ten thousand Jewish women dying of exhaustion digging a trench is whether or not the trench is completed for Germany.' And he had apparently once said to an S.S. detachment: 'You know what it's like to see a hundred Jewish corpses lying there, or five hundred, or a thousand. To have been through this and yet to have remained decent is an experience that has made us worthy members of the German race.' That was Himmler, the greatest mass murderer history has so far produced. Must I not then kill him, not only because he wanted to ruin Germany, but because he aimed to betray and destroy all values, justice, humanity and human dignity? But my family—had it not the right to live? Had I the right to destroy it by my own actions? 'He's coming now,' I thought. The door was pushed open. I grasped my pistol convulsively. Should I? Something in me contracted despairingly. Himmler walked quickly past me followed by an obsequious crew of officers. I relaxed my grip on the pistol.

§

It was August 13th. I had the dark feeling that I was going to be arrested at any moment. I paced anxiously up and down the room thinking over once again the tactics I would use to conceal the role played by the Infantry School in the uprising. I wondered if I had really talked everything over adequately with Lieutenant Goedeke and whether there weren't any sizeable gaps in my plan. Of course one thing could not be disguised: my speech and my arbitrary interference at Döberitz.

Finally I sat down to do some work. I heard a car draw up outside, a high army legal official, Herrmann, walked in and placed me under arrest. 'At least he's not an S.S. man,' I thought. In the car I asked him what was going to happen to me. 'First of all I have to take you to the Gestapo for questioning.' I asked him under no circumstances to hand me over to the Gestapo. Shrugging his shoulders he declared that as an officer I was legally only bound to appear before a court-martial but that currently the Gestapo was interfering in everything. He murmured, 'Today anything is possible.' He at any rate, he continued aloud, would do his best to have me brought before a proper court-martial. I had unpleasant forebodings. On arrival at the State Security Offices we were sent on to a subsidiary department in the Französischer Strasse. Herrmann began to look thoughtful. 'I'm not sure what I can do for you now.' On our arrival there they told him threateningly that as a 'traitor' I now belonged to the Gestapo. Herrmann quietly answered that a court-martial must first decide whether or not I was a traitor. The Gestapo man scowled and hissed at him, 'So you too want to attack us!' Herrmann came up to me and said that there now really was nothing further he could do for me. I pressed his hand and thanked him for his efforts.

I was alone. A Gestapo man in civilian clothes came along and, grinning, took away my dagger. I felt myself boiling over but controlled my feelings and resolved simply to ignore any further insults. Out in the corridor I thought over how I should behave at the interrogation. Naturally in any German court I would tell the truth, but to call the Gestapo a German court was just sarcasm.

'A government', I said to myself, 'renounces its rights when it steps beyond the bounds of law; the S.S., Hitler and Himmler are no longer our leaders. They are the gravediggers of Germany.'

The room I entered was large and bare. A typist was tapping away in the corner. An enormous desk stood in the middle of the room, and behind it in black S.S. uniform sat Sturmbannführer Krüger. Hardly had I sat down when he put the first catch question: 'You're an old soldier. Do you consider that a soldier should obey every order he is given?' I had expected this one and immediately replied: 'Of course not. A soldier should refuse to obey illegal orders'. Krüger jumped and I knew why. The answer had upset his carefully thought out game of cat and mouse; he had expected the soldier's usual reply that orders are orders and must of course be obeyed. Had I given this reply there is little doubt that he would have countered with: 'So you would be prepared to carry out illegal orders such as an order to murder the Führer.' I would have been unable to deny this and so would have given him a perfectly good reason for pronouncing me guilty because of my attitude. He tried a new tack: 'We prepared charges against you because of reports from the Döberitz Infantry School. You seized command of the School in order to hand it over to the plotters.' 'But there was an order from the Supreme Command,' I replied. Silence. Krüger digressed: 'When you went to the Bendlerstrasse you had a talk with Merz von Quirnheim. What did you talk about?' I thought quickly and realised that Merz von Quirnheim had been executed on the night of July 20th together with Stauffenberg, so I had a free hand. 'I think I asked about the general situation,' I said, without mentioning that I was the one who had suggested ordering the training battalion to the defence of the officers in the Bendlerstrasse. 'You are mistaken, Colonel. This is of course strictly a secret, but Merz von Quirnheim is alive.' I swore silently and hedged. 'After three weeks I can't remember the conversation exactly. I had to ask for authorisation as the troops were refusing to obey me.' Hardly were these words out of my mouth than he let me see that Mirz von Quirnheim had after all been shot and that I was in a trap. I managed to get out of this by talking away without getting to the point. Eventually Krüger called a halt to the interrogation. The only result was uncertainty on both sides. Krüger did not place me under arrest but held me, as the S.S. expression went, 'at their disposal.'

I slept three nights at the Gestapo. On the evening of August

16th I was suddenly arrested and driven away to the Gestapo's interrogation centre. On arrival an S.S. man came up to me, roared that it was a disgrace that a criminal should be wearing decorations, tore off my medals and felt me over for weapons or other objects. I paid no attention and gazed at a list on the wall. On this were noted the names of those under arrest: 350 men, all distinguished for their high principles, courage, honour and sense of responsibility. It was deeply moving to be in their company and I was given encouragement to stick it out. S.S. guards interrupted my contemplation and pushed me out of the room; I was taken along endless corridors. 'Here are the cells for death candidates,' mocked the S.S. man and the door closed behind me. I was alone. For a long time now my surroundings would be a narrow bunk, a stool, a pail, dirty grey walls and a tiny glazed window. I sat down on the stool and my thoughts revolved round my wife and my youngest son born on July 11th. What would happen to the little fellow after my execution? I imagined my six year old Erika radiantly taking him up in her arms, my son Wolfgang and three year old Brigitte. Had the Gestapo already struck and arrested them for being my relations? Not long before I had been told by Colonel W. that the S.S. ran the camps for relations of prisoners in much the same way as concentration camps; the worst thing of all was that children were separated from their mothers. The thought appalled me, and I began to reproach myself. Was it right to endanger my family by my actions? Was I not responsible to my family in a special way? I stared at the grey walls, sat down on the stool again and tried to see through the window pane. The baby hardly stood a chance of surviving arrest. And my wife?

Two days later the cell door opened. A jailer brought me one or two of my things—a great favour. He remarked, 'They've started to put pressure on your batman. He's going through hell for you and they've never seen anything like it in all their experience. On the whole your people seem to be right behind you. Strange,' he continued, 'yours is one of the few cases where subordinates have really stuck up for their officer when he's been arrested.' He turned away from me to go out. 'Perhaps you're not so suspect after all,' he said and shut the door.

In the next few days more news got through to me. One of my own officers let me know that shortly after my arrest my batman Heinrich had gone to my rooms and ransacked the desk and cupboards for incriminating evidence. I sighed with relief. In my haste I had not thought of this at all. Now I remembered the correspondence with the Chief of my old regiment, Prince von Hohenzollern, in which we had been less than discreet in our opinions of Hitler, his 'military genius', and the methods of the Nazis. Heinrich had been able to burn these letters just before the Gestapo took possession of my rooms. Then of course Heinrich realised the full extent of the danger I was in, and he decided to warn my family without delay. He brought my wife and children to Potsdam, near Berlin, so that they could hide from the Gestapo. At first I could hardly believe all this, but I realised that everything would be easier to endure now that I knew the family to be reasonably safe. I was fortunate in times like these to discover what it is like to have real friends. Night had fallen, and outside I could hear the steps of the S.S. guards. The cell was swarming with bugs; I crawled under the blanket, disgusted by the filthy stench. I couldn't sleep and once again went over the recent past: the evening of July 20th—the Stettin Station—I was arriving from Altwarp—met by a driver reporting the attempt on Hitler's life—my reply that I already knew—why did I have to say that? This one sentence could cost me my life. The driver would blurt it out and the S.S. would then call me a close collaborator of Stauffenburg. I had very little hope of survival.

On August 22nd I was visted by Lieutenant-Colonel Scheerle. He had succeeded me in my job and had roundly told the Gestapo that certain important problems connected with the front could not be solved without my advice. Faced with this pressure the Gestapo, after some hesitation, finally gave permission for officers of my detachment to visit me on strictly professional business. This was most unusual and I was in fact the only prisoner allowed to have visits. Scheerle told me in a low voice that all my people were right behind me. I confided to him my worry about what the driver might say. The S.S. guard approached and we began talking loudly about military matters.

The papers I had to work on were a beneficial distraction from the wearing loneliness of cell life. Now I was able to keep a diary in a little notebook. I wrote in it such items as: 'Forbidden to lie down at all during the day. Typical remark by the guards: "This isn't a sanatorium!" Bugs everywhere. The latest trick is a light burning all night above my head. My photograph taken for criminal records. On the way I see a dignified elderly clergyman being beaten up. I have put in an application as follows: "Thanks to very severe rheumatism contracted in Russia, sitting down all day is unbearably painful. I therefore ask for permission to be allowed to lie down during the day." ' It was obvious that my application would end up in someone's wastepaper basket unanswered. Everywhere there was a boundless hatred of officers which affected all of them from the most insignificant S.S. man to the highest Gestapo official. Their answers to all our pleas were torments such as making us sit motionless on a stool from 6 a.m. to 9 p.m. I felt sorry for our comrades who, chained, often tortured and beaten, forbidden to read or write, had to undergo a much harsher imprisonment.

Next day one of my officers came to fetch the papers I had been working on. He took advantage of a favourable moment to whisper to me that the driver had been interrogated. He had refused to make any statement, declaring that being hard of hearing he had not been able to follow our conversation in the car. The S.S. assumed he was lying and tortured him, but he never said a word. When he finally left the prison his hair had turned white.

In the afternoon an N.C.O. of the S.S. rushed into my cell and handcuffed me. We drove to the Alexanderplatz and I had to wait for him in the ante-room of the Gestapo Chief. My rheumatism was giving me hell. The sun shone through the open window, a great relief after the semi-darkness to which I was now accustomed. I was very hungry. There was much coming and going in the ante-room; black-uniformed S.S. men and others in civilian clothes looked at me inquisitively and grinned scornfully when they saw my handcuffs. I wondered why, but was not really concerned as I was mainly interested in my hunger. This was now so acute that from time to time everything seemed to flicker before my eyes.

I had to take a firm grip of myself in order to keep a clear head, for I knew how badly this was going to be needed. I seemed to have been in the room for an eternity. The room emptied, apparently it was suppertime: I was alone with my guard. Suddenly he stepped forward and hastily fed me a couple of rolls. Then the room filled up again. After four hours my handcuffs were removed —the interrogation would now take place in the office of Obersturmbannführer Bock. Dressed in elegant S.S. uniform Bock sat relaxed behind his desk. The first thing I noticed was a high military decoration he was wearing. 'You've never been near the front,' I thought and as a gesture of defiance greeted him with a

Heil Hitler. He noticed that this was supposed to be ironical and thundered at me, 'That is the greatest impudence I've ever come across in all my experience. Who do you think you are to drag the Hitler salute in the mud? Do you call yourself a German? You've renounced all rights to such an honourable name! You're a traitor, a murderer, a reactionary, a putschist! You are one of those who tried to stab Germany's Führer in the back!' He paused. This torrent of words was designed to scare me and knock me off balance. Now I knew that I was sitting in the presence of the Grand Inquisitor of the Third Reich. He fixed me with a cold eye, savouring the effect of his opening words and deciding that since his words had not had the desired effect, he had better draw again on his inexhaustible storm of abuse and pour it out on my head like a thunderstorm. I chanced to glance at his desk, an exaggeratedly large and important-looking one standing in the centre of the room. Bock was evidently a fanatical drinker and smoker; I began to count the bottles on the desk. 'The best thing to do is relax while he keeps raging,' I thought. 'My strength is limited and I'll need it all.' The telephone rang. It was Bock's superior, S.S. Oberführer Müller. Bock: 'We overheard some conversations, Oberführer.' His voice lost its harshness and took on a wheedling tone. 'One Major was heard to warn another . . . Certainly, Oberführer . . . Yes, of course, immediate arrest, Oberführer ! . . . Yes, Oberführer. . . he's here with me right now, we've got him where we want him, Oberführer . . . You can take the credit, Oberführer! A master-stroke !' He hung up. 'So you've got me safe and sound,' I thought. Bock was really a master of his craft; he knew how to flatter when a situation called for it and how to twist statements in such a way that something to the detriment of the accused always emerged. 'Colonel Miller !' He was calling me Miller instead of Müller; I couldn't help smirking. 'How could you possibly suppose that Himmler, the most loyal of all, should want to betray Goering? I am outraged! Entertaining the very thought is bad enough to bring you to the gallows. It is a sign of your debased mentality, Colonel Miller!' He emphasised the 'i' in Miller. I was careful not to go into the questions in detail, but said in an equally sharp tone, 'I completely deny this accusation! You're no doubt aware of the fact that the history of the National Socialist party has been one of inner struggle. I need only think of the Röhm putsch, of Gregor Strasser . . .' He interrupted me, 'That's just another sign of your baseness, Colonel Miller. How

87

can you suspect such a thing of that great man, S.S. Reichs-führer Himmler, the hero of our Fatherland? You are one of the most vicious enemies of the S.S. I have ever come across.' 'What pathos,' I thought, and put on a stern face. 'What is your attitude to the S.S.?' 'I have nothing to say,' I replied shortly. He decided to come to the point. 'So your training battalion was to occupy Oranienburg Concentration Camp!'—'Yes,' I replied, and added unasked, 'And furthermore Count Stauffenberg issued an order that after the camp had been freed the prisoners should guard the S.S.' Speechless amazement, then a loud roar. 'This order . . . was Stauffenberg's dirtiest trick of all!' Again I stared at Bock's decoration for gallantry and couldn't help grinning. What a pity, I thought, that the prisoners were after all never able to enjoy such a moment. Bock raged away. 'Who told you that Goering was out of favour with Hitler?' I replied that I had forgotten. Bock jumped to his feet and snarled, 'It's characteristic of you not to be able to remember an important fact like this. You're supposed to be an old officer, you liar!' I pulled myself together. Bock went on: 'It is characteristic of your exaggerated officer's arrogance, of your burning need for recognition, that you went to the Infantry School on July 20th. Why did you go home so very late that night?' He was clearly not expecting a reply but continued, 'And if you really had to stick your nose into it why didn't you go to the Bendler-strasse to make enquiries?' I was about to speak but he shouted, 'Don't you try and tell me anything. You're a putschist!' He drew breath, while I tried to look unconcerned and said decidedly, 'It's the Führer's command that everyone shall only know as much as is strictly necessary for the carrying out of orders.' At this he completely lost his composure, 'That's a good one! And a creature like you is still running around free!' Turning to the door he roared, 'Handcuffs!' There was now a pause as I sat before him handcuffed. My hunger was once again making itself felt. I calculated that it was now fifteen hours since my last bowl of thin soup. How late would it be now? Three a.m.? They brought Bock a glorious bowl of fruit, he peeled and ate the fruit and gave some to the typist. I chuckled inwardly. This was just like a detective story, and I remembered a book of Edgar Wallace in which some gangster or other had been softened up by the sight of rich food. My hunger was so acute that I was afraid of passing out. I kept telling myself that I must keep going and not cave in, not now when the last attack was to be expected.

Bock's next question referred to my conversation with the driver. What had I said to him? Fortunately I had heard how the brave man had kept silent and was able to avoid the trap. 'But Herr Obersturmbannführer,' I said, 'how can you suppose that I would have discussed anything with such an insignificant man?' This was intended to fit in with his picture of me as a reactionary, rank-conscious Prussian drill officer. He raged silently. I was unbelievably tired and fed up with this 'game of chess'. The need to eat and sleep was becoming unendurable. 'How do you think the war will end?' At all costs I had to avoid committing myself with my answer, so I was evasive: 'Never have the German soldier and his officer performed such deeds of heroism as in this war. Such heroic spirit is the surest foundation for Germany's future.' He lost his temper and threw me out.

In the ante-room I passed several Gestapo officials, one of whom looked up and said, 'You put him through it all right.' I was amazed. 'Don't you people stick together?', I asked. He looked at me significantly.

The days crept by. My cell was filthy beyond belief and stank unbearably; every day I hoped they would let me out into the fresh air. My lungs were so affected by lack of oxygen that I started to spit blood. Outside I could hear tired dragging footsteps accompanied by the stamping of S.S. boots, then the order: 'Turn round! Face the wall! Hands behind your neck, you traitors!' I stood up so as to listen through the door. It was hard to believe that young S.S. guards were really beating up old officers. I sat down on the stool again; my rheumatism was hurting and I was freezing cold.

The S.S. tried to break down resistance with various tricks, but even though the prisoners' bodies might weaken their inner strength could not be shaken. In the evenings there was hymn singing in some of the cells. I found great comfort in Luther's hymn 'Ein 'feste Burg ist unser Gott'. 'They're all going crazy,' said the guards.

I wrote in my diary: 'I can't stand the lack of hygiene any longer. My cell hasn't been cleaned for two weeks. I've even tried to keep the place clean by scrubbing the floor with my handkerchief.' I walked around a bit to ease the pain of the rheumatism. An S.S. guard suddenly unlocked the cell and said in a low voice, 'Colonel, we won't look through the peephole for the next two hours.' It was scarcely to be believed—were there really two human beings among the eighty S.S. men guarding us? I lay down on the bunk, for lying down eased the pain in my limbs.

In the morning a guard shouted into my cell: 'Come on you! Follow me!' In the corridor I was yelled at again and made to stand with my face to the wall. Then he took me into the courtyard where another photograph was to be taken for criminal records. I looked up at the cell windows: three elderly men raised their handcuffed wrists as a sign of greeting. How hard it must be for them, their hands bound all the time, forbidden to read or write or have visitors, continually illtreated by the S.S. I was fortunate compared with them. The guards were milder towards me because they were under the impression that I was not yet a complete outcast. I was allowed to work and to have visitors. During the night it became bitterly cold; the light above my head was switched on all the time. I tried to pull the blanket over my head. At ten p.m. one of the guards roared, 'You're only allowed to have the blanket up to your chest! Put your hands on your head!' During the night everyone was woken up twice. On September 9th they took me to a second interrogation at Police Headquarters. There I learnt that I had been denounced by Captain L. and his adjutant. Without even having been approached by the Gestapo they had reported my speech at Döberitz and my views about the outcome of the war. As a result I was once more greeted by Bock, sitting behind his desk. I admitted that the Captain's statement was to a certain extent correct, on which Bock commented, 'You stated that the assassination had been planned by the S.S.' I pretended to be shocked. 'Me? Out of the question; how could I possibly?' He was determined to make me lose my head. 'Colonel Miller, you expressed exactly the same opinions about the outcome of the war as the conspirators. They too wanted to make peace with England. You were quite clearly connected with the conspirators. Furthermore, as we all know, all previous interrogations have demonstrated your hostile attitude towards the S.S.' I looked solemn. On my way back to the prison I went over the interrogation in my mind. I calculated my chances: they were pretty small. Hostility towards the S.S.; they could bring me to the gallows for that alone.

That afternoon my human S.S. man was on duty again. I was allowed to lie down; I relaxed, whistled and thought of my wife. The next day it would be four weeks I had been in this cell, in a filthy state and bitten all over by bugs, four weeks during which the thought of Germany's fate never left me, four weeks under perpetual fear of death. For a long time I thought deeply about my family. I discovered what it meant to have the thought of a merciful God always with me in the face of death.

There followed several further interrogations. I knew they were asking Lieutenant Goedeke the same questions as myself in order to get us to contradict one another. Fortunately before my arrest Goedeke and I had gone over our answers to the most various questions in great detail. After the interrogations I realised that we had not covered everything and this worried me considerably. I brooded as to how I might let him know about my statements and wrote them down on a piece of paper. The following afternoon the visit of Major Ludwig of the infantry was announced. 'That's splendid,' I thought. The guard brought me into the visiting room. I sat opposite Ludwig and discussed various documents with him. Eventually the S.S. man on guard stood up to bring our conversation to an end. 'Now or never,' I thought, and got up nervously. The guard stood at the door waiting. I pretended to be polite and said, 'After you, gentlemen. You're my guests.' The S.S. guard was so flattered by this that he happily strutted on ahead. In a flash I pressed the bit of paper on Ludwig and hurried after the S.S. man. Ludwig said goodbye to me. I sat down contentedly on my stool and heard the guard saying to Ludwig as they walked off, 'I oughtn't really to have gone on ahead. The Colonel could have easily passed you a message. But the Colonel's harmless.'

The next morning an S.S. chief inspector asked me abruptly whether there was anything I wanted. I was so astonished that at first I said nothing, then I asked for a broom. He went away. What had happened? Was everything going to be all right after all? That evening I was moved to another cell, a clean one, but I soon noticed that I had made a bad exchange. There was no blanket. When I asked for one, the guard shouted, 'Shut up, or I'll belt you one, you traitor!' In the night the sirens wailed: an air raid on Berlin. All hell was let loose in the prison. Loud clanking of keys and curses; the S.S. guards ran from cell to cell to lock us in. One could hear the humming and whining of the aeroplanes followed by the thud of explosions, some of them quite close. The thick walls shuddered and glass smashed. My little window pane was broken and a cold draught blew in. I prepared myself for a sleepless night in the icy cold, with rheumatism and spitting blood. The guards were shouting again in the corridor. One of them came in and told me I had been acquitted. I couldn't believe my ears. I tried to sleep a bit despite the cold. 'Tomorrow I'll be free and will be able to go to Potsdam,' I thought. I had just dozed off when the guard shouted through the peephole, 'Hands above your head, Colonel!'

The next morning there was a joyful meeting outside the prison office. Seven of my fellow prisoners had been released at the same time as myself. A prison van took us for one more visit to the State Security Office. A crowd of Berliners collected as we emerged. They looked on with silent amazement at the sight of officers coming out of the 'Green Minna', as they called the police vans. Leaving the State Security Office I crossed the Tiergarten. I felt my legs about to give way and was overcome by faintness, so had to sit down on a bench.

Like me, my wife had been convinced that we would never see each other again. On my arrival in Potsdam the children rushed up to me joyfully; she stood somewhat aside, and we were happy. After only a few hours I received a telegram from the Personnel Office which ordered me to the front until April 1st for a period of probation; failing this I would be reduced to the ranks. This procedure was the greatest slight on his honour a soldier could receive. It was now made impossible for me to become a general. In any case I was ordered to return to the front, which in my present state of health meant suicide. I had myself examined by a doctor who at once transferred me to the hospital at Bad Pyrmont; here I slowly began to recover from my lung trouble. Meanwhile the S.S. were on my tracks and I was ordered to compile training manuals for the Home Guard. Once again I was confronted by an impossibly difficult decision; Hitler had called for total defence in order that Germany might, as he proclaimed, win the war by bitter partisan fighting. He had instructed the Gauleiters to call up everyone from 16 year old youths to old men of 70. To give weapons to 16 year olds and send them to fight a trained enemy was a murderous crime; and I was expected to lend my knowledge and experience to this senseless plan in a war that was already lost. I had no choice but to refuse this order. But I knew that a blank refusal would inevitably bring further Gestapo imprisonment, and I had scarcely a chance of surviving it. I considered how I might play for time, and wrote a memorandum setting out all the disadvantages of the Home Guard plan. Of course this was not at all what Himmler's people wanted to hear, and they began to put further pressure on me. At my wit's end, I eventually consulted the hospital doctor. He reflected for a moment, then telephoned S.S. Headquarters, telling them that Colonel Müller would not be able to carry out the instructions they had issued as his health had taken a considerable turn for the worse. So that I could avoid being checked up on further he transferred me to the lung hospital at Bad Münder. But here too the S.S. gave me no rest. One day they rang' up and demanded that I be handed over to the S.S. Punishment Battalion. There was no more escape. I went to say goodbye to the doctor. 'Unfortunately there's nothing I can do for you,' he said; 'As an old Social Democrat I am expecting arrest any day.' I returned to my room; I was done for. A nun came in and asked if she should make my bed. 'No thanks,' I replied, 'there wouldn't be any point. I'm just about to be taken away by the S.S.' She looked scared. 'Why is that?' 'I made some anti-S.S. speeches on July 20th and now they want to kill me in the S.S. Punishment Battalion!' 'That—that's not right,' she said, 'now, such a short time before the end of the war.' She reflected for a moment, made a despairing face, walked indecisively out of the door, but quickly came back. 'Get into bed quickly, I will save you.' A car drew up below. She ran to the window and said, 'They're coming.' Then she took my sputum and exchanged it with that of a man who was dying of tuberculosis. Talking loudly two S.S. officials came up the stairs. The nun went out of my room leaving the door ajar. The S.S. men wanted to speak to the doctor, but he had prudently gone off to visit another hospital in the neighbourhood. They showed the nun their orders for my removal. 'But that's out of the question. Colonel Müller is extremely ill with tuberculosis.' They thereupon demanded to see me. 'You can't do that,' she said quietly, 'you'd be infected. But I can show you the sputum and the doctor's report. She came in; I kept my eyes shut and lay motionless. Then she disappeared again, closing the door. After a while car doors were slammed down below. They had gone!

§

It was the first of April. Since in the intervening period I had failed to undergo my 'probation' at the front I was now automatically degraded to the ranks. I therefore went to the senior army doctor in the hospital to have my epaulettes removed. He refused and said that to do anything of that sort would be completely immoral. He wanted to have nothing to do with such a criminal system. So that the S.S. might not find me so easily he sent me to a small hospital nearby at Coppenbrügge.

The hospital had originally been a private nursing home. On the ground floor there were between thirty and forty men back from the front, mostly badly wounded, and seven officers on the first floor. In the first few weeks I talked with the soldiers to find out their attitude towards the Nazis. A Corporal, Anton Frohnapfel, was particularly disapproving: the Nazis would shirk wherever there was real danger and push the soldiers forward. Their convictions were not worth much.

One day we found an order from the Gauleiter of Hanover affixed to the wall. All hospitals in the Hanover district were to resist the invaders to the last man. I could only shake my head. The wounded, the maimed, women and old men were expected to take up arms against the advancing British. What utter madness. Although I had in theory lost my rank I assembled all the patients in the hospital together. I explained the Gauleiter's order and myself directed that the hospital was to keep to the Geneva Convention: hospitals should not be defended with arms, all weapons should be locked away. My instructions were followed. I then paid a secret visit to the local priest; I told him that it was sheer lunacy to expose Coppenbrügge and its hospitals to shooting, we could only defend ourselves for two hours at the most with our weapons, and to sacrifice human lives for those two hours would be senseless and wrong. He agreed completely and it was decided that he was to hoist a white sheet on the church tower as soon as the British appeared. As I left the priest's house troops were marching through the main street of the village. My plan for saving the village and its inhabitants seemed to have foundered already. I went to have a word with the Captain in charge, but none of my humane arguments had the slightest effect. He merely repeated over and over again that he had instructions from the highest quarters to defend the village at all costs. This type of officer was well known to me, so I roared at him, 'You've no business to obey orders blindly. You should think. Look,' I pointed to the position that the soldiers were to occupy directly in front of the village, 'from a military point of view it is quite crazy to take up position here. You can see that we are in a valley; when the enemy approaches he'll attack at once from the hills behind and there will be no possibility of withdrawal.' He realised this, but still hesitated. However, eventually he withdrew and evacuated the village.

Needless to say my interference with the Gauleiter's authority was not without consequences. That evening the senior doctor of the Hanover district was telephoned by the Gauleiter who raged about a mad Colonel who had thrown the troops out of the village. Morning came. I was just leaving my room on the first floor when I observed three S.S. men down below who were talking with both my room neighbours, two Captains. I heard that they had been sent to arrest me by the Gauleiter. My hand closed round the pistol in my trouser pocket; if necessary I would defend myself with it—now of all times, just before the end of the war, I had no intention of allowing myself to be shot according to martial law. The two captains gave my room number and disappeared; I stood waiting at my door. Apparently several of the soldiers had been silently listening to the conversation, for Anton Frohnapfel suddenly planted himself before the S.S. men and said, 'What do you want here? You want to take the Colonel away? Not on your life!' He stepped aside and threw the doors open, 'Come on out, all of you. These bastards want to take the Colonel away. We can't allow that, can we?' The entrance hall slowly filled with soldiers, one with his leg in plaster, another with his arm in a sling, a third with a bandaged head. They were all muttering and cursing. 'You with your smart uniforms, you've never had to lie in the mud, you shirking bastards.' Frohnapfel spoke again, 'Yes, you shirking bastards. Go to the front, to the Russian marshes with bullets whistling round your ears, and when you've done that come again and fetch the Colonel.' The S.S. men looked uneasy and moved back before the threatening crowd of wounded soldiers. 'If you don't scram now, we'll make you. Hey, Fritz, bring the pistol,' he said to his neighbour, 'we'd better show them that they can't just take away a Colonel from us like that.' The situation was getting threatening and the abuse louder. 'Let them have it!' shouted the bedridden soldiers from the wards. The S.S. men looked at each other uncertainly and left the hospital. The group of soldiers pursued them with scornful abuse and advised them not to let themselves be seen again.

§

Hitler had committed suicide, the Commander-in-Chief of the German Army signed a document of unconditional surrender, and German troops went into captivity. The civilian population started painfully trying to build a new future out of the ruins. The past twelve years weighed on them like a bad dream and they repeatedly asked themselves the same horrified question: how could all this have happened?

But people are not willing to contemplate the terrible past for too long; rather do they preoccupy themselves with the present and its manifold distractions. But the past had come so close to me that I still cannot be free of it. One problem has become a fundamental question for me: how can a system based on terror be effectively combatted? I had all too clearly perceived that it was virtually impossible to overthrow a tyranny from inside. For every dictator maintains a network of secret police, deceives the people with one-sided propaganda and raises the standard of living at the expense of 'inferior races' in order to tame the will of the people. By these methods he keeps the people for ever on the edge of the abyss. Who can then restrain him?

I therefore consider that a conflagration must be extinguished in the very first stages, that a dictatorship must be stamped on at the outset and that it is our duty to protect the democratic state at all times, particularly in grave economic crises.

How easily do we allow the results of elections to comfort us in times of peace and quiet, and how easily are we taken in by the refined psychological tricks of demagogues—and before we know where we are they have the reins of power in their hands! Then the same thing always happens: the honest citizen creeps into his shell in order to survive: he neither actively supports the ruling party nor does he oppose the system. In this he is merely motivated by common sense. But it is my opinion that a human being, and especially a Christian, cannot be expected to limit his activity if he lives under an unjust government, should he wish to remain really guiltless. Whether we admit it or not we are responsible for what Hitler did to the Jews. And the excuse that any intervention against Hitler would have been senseless will not hold water, since the value of an action motivated by a sense of responsibility should never be determined by the chances of success. The only criterion that should determine my actions is the obligation to be true to that which God demands from the individual—regardless of public opinion, regardless of the chances of success.

It is my personal belief that God demands action, that He wants a resistance which is the rebellion of the conscience. And the German resistance to Hitler was such a rebellion.

POLAND

Waclaw Zagorski

Some events from the family history loomed particularly large in my childhood. One of these was mentioned rarely and only in passing—the fact that my father's younger sister had spent quite a few years in a Tsarist prison for taking part in the 1905 revolution. Occasionally someone would say: 'When Maria was in the Lukian-ówka prison . . .' or: 'That was before Maria's trouble . . .' and then the atmosphere in the room would grow quiet and solemn for a moment. The walls were covered with prints showing the Russian execution of the members of the National Government on the slopes of the Warsaw Citadel in 1864 and the prison coaches taking the Polish insurgents to Siberia under Cossack escort.

Another piece of family history concerned my father, who was at the gala performance in the Theatre at Kiev, when his friend, a Russian lawyer, shot the Tsarist minister Stolypin. An eminent Polish surgeon called Makowski was ordered to extract the bullet from the victim's brain, under the watchful eyes of a group of Russian doctors. Late that night, after he had finished the opera-tion, Doctor Makowski went to the Polish Club, where his friends were awaiting him. He answered my father's question by saying, 'The operation was a success. The doctors present congratulated me and expressed their admiration. But Stolypin's condition need arouse no anxiety. He will be dead in a few hours. . . .' And so it turned out. Makowski was a frequent guest at my parents' home.

My mother told us of one such event which had taken place before the first world war at a summer resort near Kiev. One day, guided by chance or the instinct of a hunted beast, a man who had broken away from a prison convoy took refuge in my grandmother's villa. A minute later some Russian police ran after him on to the veranda. At the front door stood a frail old woman in black, blocking their way.

'A bandit just ran in here,' shouted the oldest of the pursuers.

'Nobody has come in here,' said my grandmother firmly.

'But we saw him.'

'You are mistaken. Please leave.'

Today it is hard to imagine how, in the great expanses of the Russian Empire, anyone could talk to the police in such a manner; but in this respect the Tsarist police were somewhat backward.

The fugitive had been crouching just behind the door. Neither then nor later were any questions asked of him. He was given a workman's clothes and the next day appeared in the yard in the guise of an itinerant worker newly hired to chop wood. After a week or so he thanked my grandmother and left, his real name still unknown.

My mother probably never knew just what were the aims of the Bolsheviks, of whom this fugitive was one, or of the Mensheviks, to whom my father belonged. And to this day she couldn't give a clear answer if asked what the Polish Social Democrats want, although her son is one. Having told us this story she said to us in a self-justificatory tone, 'One must help anyone who is being persecuted by those who are stronger than he, anyone who is defenceless and being pursued by armed men. . . .'

In later years I never again heard my mother speak such words aloud. But shortly after that there began an almost daily procession of fugitives seeking shelter—deserters from the Russian army; wounded Polish legionaires from General Haller's brigade after its battle near Kaniow; Germans and Russians fleeing after the capture of Kiev by the Socialist Petlura in his fight to achieve an independent Ukraine; Petlura's own men in flight from the Bolsheviks; Bolsheviks trapped by Denikin's forces attempting to restore Tsarist rule. And again, twenty years later in Warsaw my mother would hide in her Zoliborz house Home Army soldiers and Jews whom I had sent to her because they were hotly pursued not only by the Nazi oppressors but by Polish and even Jewish traitors who worked with them. During these times her eyes never lost that look of self-justification, as if she was saying to the worried neighbours who feared not only for her life but for their own, 'After all, one must help anyone who is being persecuted. . . .'

I had a dramatic reminder of the story of that nameless refugee in our summer villa near Kiev on 6th January, 1920, when Poland had regained her independence after 130 years of foreign rule. My mother and I had come to Warsaw as refugees from the Ukraine, now overrun by the Bolsheviks. On that memorable day my father, whom we had given up for dead, suddenly appeared in our little room in the south-eastern division of the Polish Red Cross.

He had been arrested in June 1919 by the Bolsheviks as a Socialist and a member of the Central Polish Committee in the Ukraine and put in the dungeons of the Kiev Cheka. We had heard reports that the man who had been arrested with my father, Pereswiet Soltan, the Chairman of the Polish Committee, a person of high ideals, leader of the progressive lawyers in Kiev, and, like my father, a selfless defender of political prisoners in the Tsarist courts, had been executed; and that many other Polish and Russian Mensheviks had been murdered at the same time. We had received no news of my father for many months, so how could we have hoped that he was still alive?

But here he was now, having tracked us down over a thousand miles from Kiev. He was ragged, emaciated, lousy but alive. He told us how he had managed to escape.

After a long period of interrogation and torture in the basement cells of the Kiev gaol, and having several times been stood up against a wall that was spattered with the blood and brain fragments of executed prisoners, my father was taken out of his cell one night. But instead of being led to the basement dungeons or to the prison yard where executions were carried out, he was taken outside the town. There, in a deserted place, stood the ruins of a thatched mud hut, uninhabited and unrepaired like many in the Ukraine, about which the local peasants would spin legends of hanged men, infanticides and souls doing penitence. The Chekist who led the convoy halted the militiamen and, with his revolver cocked, took my father inside himself.

'You don't recognise me,' he said to my father in a low voice, 'but I recognised you at once. I told them that I had an old score to settle with you and they agreed that I should deal with you. Here's a pass and behind the chimney stack you'll find a wood-cutter's clothes and tools and some bread. Your mother once saved my life. If she's still alive, tell her I've paid off my debt. . . .'

He shot several times at the crumbling wall and went out.

To this very day I should probably have regarded this story as a naïve little morality tale for children but for the fact, that years later, when I was putting my father's desk in order after his death I found a carefully preserved document bearing witness to human gratitude—a pass written in pencil on a small piece of poor-quality paper and stamped with the primitive seal of the Kiev security commission. Moreover, my own later experiences were to convince me that the most fantastic encounters were possible on the crooked paths of man's fate.

In the third week of the German invasion of Poland, the Red Army invaded Polish territory from the East, in conformity with the secret pact between Stalin and Hitler. On that day, 17th September, 1939, I was in the town of Luck, in Eastern Poland, having been called up as a reserve officer. The Polish units were retreating southwards towards Lwow and the Hungarian border, along the narrow strip of territory left between the German army attacking from the West and the Soviet 'liberators' advancing from the East. I was ordered to stay in the city as long as possible with the town's military commander, Colonel Haberling; our job was to secure the bridges over the Styr and to protect the thousands of refugees in the town and the local civilian population from the looting that was beginning in the chaos of defeat; there were also scores of German prisoners-of-war to be safeguarded against the threat of lynching.

On 18th September the first armoured column of the Soviet army passed through the city under the command of Major Klimov. After that we were again left on our own in Luck; Polish flags were still flying over the barracks that had been destroyed by the German air force and over the temporary H.Q. of the local military command in an office building in the city centre.

Next day the Soviet infantry entered the city. The commander asked us to come to his quarters in the municipal building, to work out a joint plan for the evacuation (whither to?) of refugees, prisoners-of-war and wounded from the overcrowded hospitals.

I had orders from Colonel Haberling to go along with him. We walked straight into a trap. In the antechamber of the city town hall heavily-armed Red Army men surrounded us. We had only side-arms. We were immediately ordered to strip, and subjected to a detailed and lengthy search, after which only our trousers, tunics and boots were returned to us. They even kept our underwear, saying, 'You won't need that any more.'

Then we were brought up before a court-martial on the charge of 'preparing an armed uprising against the Soviet Union in the rear of the Red Army'.

In the military council chamber, the tribunal was presided over by the regimental *politruk* (political officer). The Red Army assassins came and went in rapid succession, but there was also a regular 'local adviser' in the shape of a young law student called Ettinger, the son of a rich paper-merchant; on the previous day he had become the first commander of the Workers' Guard of Luck.

Ettinger and I knew each other well. Some years before the war he used to write sports notes for a paper which I edited. One day he was arrested by the Polish police on a charge of belonging to the illegal Communist Party of the Western Ukraine. I was outraged at this. I was not a communist but I had always fought for freedom of conscience, conviction, expression and association. The curtailing of these freedoms in one's own country in peacetime was exceptionally painful to me and to every Pole who still cherished the traditions of fighting against tyranny for the sake not only of narrowly conceived national ideals but of broader human values. The number of political prisoners at that time was growing and this intensified one's feelings of solidarity with them as against the police, the guardians of order and security, who increasingly tended to descry communism in every manifestation of independent and progressive thought.

This climate of opinion was enhanced by the growing frequency and blatancy with which the police forces abused their authority. At every trial of a communist in Wolynia a man called Zareba was called as an expert and a competent witness for the prosecution. He was a former director of the bureau of investigation in Luck, whose name had achieved some notoreity following a parliamentary question raised by the left-wing parties about the beating of political prisoners during questioning. I still remember to this day a sentence about this affair from the political article which my father wrote in the weekly publication of the Wolynian Democratic Association: 'Poland will not be *beaten* into shape. Human rights are sacred.' The Minister of the Interior, General Slawoj Skladkowski, came to Luck in person; after returning to the capital he was compelled to make a statement in parliament that, after ascertaining that abuses had occurred, he had dismissed the staff of the local bureau of investigation. But the weekly which my father edited was closed down and Zareba, officially dismissed from the service, got some lucrative licenses for running bus services, stayed on in Luck, and went on beating suspects. And right up to September 1939 his word alone in the court decided the fate of hundreds of people charged with activities against the State.

When it came to Ettinger's case I took a firm line. I was convinced of his innocence, and after countless approaches to various officials and repeated personal meetings with the provincial governor of Wolynia, Jozewski, I managed to get him released from prison and have his case quashed. Now Ettinger sat before me as my judge. Now his word alone decided the life or death of those who had been caught in the town and of the growing numbers of Polish policemen and officials and Ukrainian nationalists who were being brought before this improvised court-martial. The Ukrainian nationalists got the shortest shrift. It was enough for Ettinger to say, 'another of the nationalist canaille' and the *politruk* would, without further questions, make an unmistakable sign to the waiting riflemen.

After two hours Colonel Haberling was taken out. At that time I regarded his fate as sealed, but he must have survived this court, for after the war I found his name on the list of identified bodies which had been recovered from the mass graves of Polish officers murdered by the NKWD in 1940 in the Katyn Woods, on Stalin's orders.

The fight for my life lasted eight hours, virtually without any participation from me. It was Ettinger who fought cleverly and discreetly. He did not win it but did succeed in getting the decision deferred. The *politruk*, growing weary, yawned a few times, got up and said to me with a smile, 'All right then. I'll think it over again. And you'll have time to do some thinking as well.'

He gave orders for me to be taken to the prison, from which the communists had been released two days ago.

§

Well after midnight the cell door opened, and a military plain-clothes militiaman with a red band on his sleeve and a rifle slung over his shoulder called my name. I went into the brightly-lit corridor, where two more militiamen were waiting. In the prison courtyard stood a saloon car which had, until a few days ago, belonged to the provincial governor's office. Now its bonnet was adorned with a red streamer with a hammer and sickle on it, the mark of the new authorities. The militiamen motioned me to get into the back seat and got in on either side. The car started off, somebody opened the prison gate, the guard at the gate saluted and we drove off into the familiar but deserted streets of Luck.

The militiaman who was sitting by the driver suddenly turned round and asked me:

'Where shall we take you, Sir?'

'Perelmutter!'

It was only now that I recognised him. And the driver was a Ukranian called Bokuc—both of them friends of mine, compositors from the State printing-house in Luck.

'Where should you take me? How on earth do I know?'

'Well, if you don't know where to go, Commandant Ettinger told us to take you to Dr. Rafalowski. You'll be safe there. You're lucky, Sir. The regiment that was here yesterday has moved forward. The court chairman left all the records with Ettinger, to be handed to the one who'll take over tomorrow. The Commandant said that you should try to get some civilian clothes at once. He'll come and see you himself tomorrow.'

Ettinger was as good as his word. First of all, he gave back every penny of the money which had been taken from me during the search, not only my own money but also a large sum which was the residue of the funds belonging to the city's military command. He also brought me a pass, made out by himself and stamped with the seal 'Workers' Guard of Luck'. This pass was written in Ukrainian and read 'Comrade Waclaw Zagorski has lost his identification papers; this is to certify his identity.'

This document was amazingly like the pass which my father had got from the Kiev security commission twenty years earlier. But it was written on a rather larger piece of paper and in ink.

§

Ettinger was not to know how many needy people would be helped by the money which he had restored to me. He certainly did not suppose that amongst other uses this money would make it possible for a secret Socialist printing press to be set up in Wilno, right under the nose of the Soviet garrison, after the lapse of only a few weeks; or that on this printing press a Polish compositor from Warsaw would be setting and printing a paper which I initiated and called *Freedom*. Ettinger would not have believed that the document he issued was to save me, ten months later, not from the Communists but from the Gestapo. This was during an attempt to cross the border between German occupied territory into the Soviet zone illegally at night. I was caught on the barbed wire and put into gaol at Danilow. With only this one piece of paper that I could safely show, I was able to convince my German interrogators that I was not a Pole but a Ukrainian and a Communist and thus—at that time—an ally. But Ettinger must have realised that he was giving me a pass to the underground, from which he himself had come only a few days earlier—the underground which would now be fighting against him and his principals and against the oppressive force that they represented and were using in these territories.

§

I have asked myself more than once what motives inspired the Chekist in Kiev in 1919 and the Commandant of the Communist militia in Luck in 1939. Were they the same? Was it just plain human gratitude for help given to them at a time when they themselves were defenceless and hunted by armed men because of their convictions? Was it perhaps a subconscious desire to free themselves from a disagreeable debt, whose very existence was jarring and weakening, even though there was no necessity to repay it? Or simply the sort of impulse which at times would cause even a German S.S. man, during the murder of hundreds of innocent victims, to let a single Jewish child escape from a ghetto that was being liquidated. Some of these criminals would not admit even to themselves having felt such human impulses, but called them their 'whims' or found in them a means of satisfying an unfulfilled power complex which they could not gratify in their own units. Others, on the contrary, would afterwards sentimentalise over their own soft-heartedness.

These reflexions however came later. When I left Luck after several days' hiding in a friend's house, I wore some trousers hastily bought which were too wide for me and a jacket which was part of a detective's costume from the Wolynian Theatre.

I carried a small suitcase and Ettinger's pass in my pocket. I was travelling in a hired peasant cart with two doctors whom I met by chance. Nevertheless even then, over and above the fresh memories of the war that was burning out so quickly here, of the first bombs falling on Warsaw, of villages and towns in flames, of corpses in the roadside ditches, of choking fear under machine-gun fire—I was aware that now, apart from an instinct for survival which circumstances had made sharper and more alert, I was bound by no obligations other than loyalty to myself.

In the course of a few days my pre-war place of work had ceased to exist, the institutions and associations to which I belonged had crumbled, as had the army to which I had been called up. I had neither supervisors nor subordinates. All dates and deadlines had been cancelled. The laws which I recognised had ceased to be binding, and I had neither the inclination nor the capacity to conform to the new ones. I was no longer an editor, or chairman of a journalists' union, or an army officer. I was just myself. I did not even have a definite goal or direction in my journeying. I was being hunted, but I was free as never before. Even from fear.

§

Freedom stimulates thought. Freedom gives one a feeling of responsiblity for one's own words and actions.

In October I reached Wilno, after being hidden by my uncle, a Social Democrat of long standing, in a game-keeper's cottage on the Wilejka river, some miles from the city. Now I in my turn passed as a wood-cutter, driving into Wilno with a load of firewood. In the city, which was crowded with refugees from the Nazi invasion and being terrorised and plundered by the Red Army, I met friends and acquaintances from all parts of Poland. Moving stealthily about in the shadows, these were people who were free in the same way as myself. We exchanged thoughts about the past, the present and the future. About the war, the defeat, the fate of Poland, the barbarities committed by the victors of the day. No one regarded our defeat as final, no one wished to capitulate or to wait for deliverance from the West. All were seeking ways in which to carry on the fight.

Out of these conversations came the 'Freedom Manifesto' which I drafted in early November 1939. I wrote:

> After twenty years of existence as an independent state Poland has become the victim of the imperialism and unparalleled aggression of

Nazi Germany. The Republic's territories have been occupied by foreign armies, bringing with them violence and lawlessness. Europe has been plunged into the abyss of war . . . Nazi Germany has forced this war on the world to achieve its aims against the imperialistic interests of England and France. But in addition to its imperialistic character this war has another aspect: it is a war between Hitlerism and democracy, between totalitarianism, barbarism, cultural and moral brutalisation on the one hand and the ideals of freedom and justice on the other. This is the essence of this war as it is seen by the ordinary people not only in oppressed Poland but in England and France as well.

Nazism must go under in this war. But the victory of the Allies cannot mean the hegemony of some states over others. A new Europe must emerge from the chaos of war, organised on the principles of political freedom and social justice. This is the Europe that is desired by millions of people and by the servicemen fighting on all fronts.

The Freedom Manifesto then declared that Poland would continue to fight despite her military defeat, and called upon the working masses of Poland to carry on this struggle to ultimate victory, in accordance with the nation's century-and-a-half-old tradition of fighting for independence and democracy. For Poland the aims of the struggle were formulated in the following ten points:

1. The principal aim of this struggle for the Polish working masses is to rebuild Poland's political independence.

2. The political system and socio-economic structure of Poland must once and for all exclude the existence of privileged social groups which aspire to get control of the political and economic power.

3. The government of Poland must be based on the principles of political democracy, to be guaranteed by the following conditions: a popular electoral system based on electoral laws enforcing a secret ballot, and an equal, universal, direct and proportional representation; a government responsible to parliament; an independent judiciary; a wide range of autonomy for local government; freedom of speech, the press, assembly and party association; and personal inviolability for all citizens.

4. The influence of large-scale capitalists and landowners on the destiny of Poland must be removed by the liquidation of large

private estates by means of complete and immediate agrarian reforms, by nationalising or establishing strict national controls over the banks and the larger industrial establishments, and by extending support to small farmers and co-operatives, and protection to small businesses.

5. Poland's armed forces must have a solid democratic basis, and any form of military caste system rendered impossible.

6. All minorities in Poland must be guaranteed equal rights, political, economic and cultural. Racialism and anti-Semitism must be eradicated from public life in Poland.

7. The demand for free and universal education for all citizens must be met.

8. Scientific and religious freedoms must be assured.

9. All citizens of the new Poland must be assured of protective labour laws, a public health service and the right to work. It is essential to develop a system of national insurance based on co-operative management.

10. Poland's foreign policy must be based on a close co-operation and fraternal understanding with all the free peoples of the world, and in particular with the nations with which she is called upon to live in neighbourly concord.

The manifesto ended with the words:

To fight for such a Poland is to fight for freedom, justice and peace. To fight for such a Poland is to fight for socialism. In this fight the working masses of Poland are not isolated. They are in the same camp as the working masses of the whole world, against the totalitarianism that is bringing chains and ruin to the peoples of Europe. In fighting for Poland's freedom, we are fighting for the destinies of all the oppressed nations. We are fighting under our fine and traditional battle cry: For your freedom and ours.

§

Those were the first and the last words that I wrote during the war years. Only after the war was over did I learn, from reading material published in the West, that my 'Freedom Manifesto' had been recognised as the earliest attempt to formulate a short programme for the struggle of the Polish Socialist Party in the new conditions resulting from the German and Soviet occupations. But that was not important. What was important was that the ten friends to whom I read the manifesto at a secret meeting decided to set up an underground Social-Democratic organisation under the name 'Freedom', of which they would form the central committee and I would direct the executive. Moreover, shortly after that, the manifesto itself which was printed by the most primitive methods in a secret printing-shop in a house in the railwaymen's housing estate in Wilno was to discover an unexpectedly large number of supporters.

These supporters swore an oath of secrecy and loyalty to me, as I had been the first to do to the ten members of the Central Committee. At carefully arranged secret meetings professors, lawyers, economists, writers, actors, students, artisans, labourers, officers, n.c.o's and soldiers who had evaded imprisonment or escaped from the internment camps in Lithuania, would intently repeat after me, whom they now knew only by the nom-de-guerre of Daniel, these words: 'I swear to devote all my strength to the rebuilding of Poland's independence and the liberation of the working masses, not to begrudge my blood and my life for my country and cause, to obey the decisions and orders of the officers of 'Freedom', and always to remain loyal to the Freedom Manifesto in a future free Poland.'

Through the city streets marched Red Army columns in close ranks, sometimes drowning the words of the oath with their strong voices singing the military song: 'If there is war tomorrow, if there is a march tomorrow . . .' or 'I know no other place where a man can breathe so freely. . . .'

Wilno's prisons were overflowing. On the railway sidings trains were being loaded with the equipment of entire factories, with the contents of archives and museum collections. On other sidings N.K.W.D. men were putting wire round and sealing up carriages full of people who were being taken into the depths of Russia, to the Siberian labour-camps and collective farms.

§

After I had organised a code liaison system with Paris and London via Stockholm I handed over the direction of the now developed organisation in Wilno to Antoni Panski, a man older than myself, an economist and sociologist, and the translator of Bertrand Russell's works into Polish. I then left Wilno with several copies of the first number of our secret paper *Freedom*, and made my way through as many as four patrol cordons to Warsaw. I was greeted by the sight of streets still not cleared of rubble and empty black eyeholes of windows in burnt-out apartment buildings. The poverty among the people and the patrols of hefty German military police with their heavy boots, helmets, rifles, belts hung with hand-grenades and their arrogant mien were a constant reminder that Poland's defeat in September was synonymous with the triumph of tyranny and boorishness.

Some months earlier I had sent a comrade with the pseudonym 'Bogumil' ahead of me from Wilno to Warsaw. He had already succeeded in setting up the first cell of the Freedom Movement, and had arranged contacts with those Polish Socialist Party members who were active in the capital, and with the military organisers of the underground army. Almost the very day of Warsaw's surrender the nucleus of a central command for the resistance movement was formed. This was composed of representatives of the main political parties. There was also the efficient high command of the Union for Armed Combat (ZWZ), later to become the underground Home Army. And there were several dozen underground groups of all political colours and different spheres of activity, which had sprung up in the same spontaneous way as 'Freedom'. Moreover, the underground newspapers were already being secretly circulated and helping to maintain the spirit of resistance.

In spite of all this activity the Freedom Manifesto became an avowal of faith and a source of hope for many people in Warsaw as well. It is astonishing how people in the underground find and recognise one another in the labyrinth of a city of a million people, even though they are living under false names in hideouts known to nobody, often with their whole appearance changed beyond recognition, eluding police and the hordes of agents and *agents provocateurs*. And how often one can, in a crowd of plain, everyday people, who in normal circumstances would have passed their entire lives uneventfully as ordinary bread-winners, find a willing and responsible person to perform even the most difficult and dangerous tasks for the sake of freedom. As the current of underground life and underground struggle began to flow wider and faster it set more and more tasks—so the organisation of the Freedom Movement continued to grow, despite the original decision to limit the number of members and to be highly selective about their quality. The new intake included soldiers of the underground army who had already taken the oath.

Some of these showed particular talent, industry and knowledge of character in organising the underground groups of five, among whom intensive ideological and technical training was propounded. Others monitored the radio stations or organised a smooth-running network for distributing the underground press. Others again became specialists in preparing microfilms to be smuggled through to the West, in encoding letters and telegrams or in forging all sorts of documents from birth certificates and Aryan identity cards for Jews to German work-permits, passports and travel-passes for the liaison officers and special messengers who had to cross the frontiers. Increasing numbers of people were needed to organise assistance for prisoners, or to hide Jews and comrades who had been flushed out by the police. There was no lack of volunteers. There were, however, some jobs for which I found it harsh to allocate people.

One of these was to move the heavy suitcases full of Jewish underground newspapers from the Warsaw ghettos to the Jewish districts in all the larger towns of the 'General Government' and those Polish Western territories which had been incorporated into the Reich. This had to be done by train and the trains were subjected to thorough searches. Out of the numerous volunteers I chose an actress called Maria Szczesna, who was no longer young. I only did this after a comrade who was a doctor in the Cancer Institute had certified that she had cancer of the womb and had not much longer to live. She carried out her task marvellously, pretending to be German, flirting with German officers and sometimes getting them to help her place her suitcases on the luggage-rack in the special compartments *nur für Deutsche*—only for Germans—which were not searched. She was not caught for several months, but finally fell into the hands of the Gestapo during a search at the station in Piotrkow.

Nina Veidt, a lovely young drama student from the State Institute of Dramatic Art, was assigned without undue hesitation to a job which was much less dangerous, or so it seemed to me. But after a couple of weeks she was arrested for complicity in hiding British airmen who had been shot down by the Germans and later escaped from prisoner-of-war camps. She was sentenced to death by a court in Berlin.

§

There were thousands of such people, who in the war against tyranny were willing to and did sacrifice their lives for freedom.

It would not, however, be true if I were to suggest, for the sake of false national pride, that the Polish people were all such people. It is true that the Poles in their struggle against Fascism and Nazism did not produce a single Quisling at the highest level of their political hierarchy. But even in Poland the Germans did not find it too difficult to recruit pocket Quislings and common traitors, *agents provocateurs* and informers. I knew a few of these people well before the war and was to encounter some of them again underground.

§

There was a Polish police sergeant called Muraszko who was later a security officer in the district administration office at Rowne; he had many friends among politicians and civil servants, especially those of the younger generation. He met one of these, Leon Stachorski, in the street, and arranged to meet him in a small café. The two men met at the appointed time and place. After greeting Stachorski and looking round the room, where he saw nobody he knew, Muraszko went to the telephone, then came back to the table. Five minutes later armed Germans in uniform came into the café. They did not ask to see anybody's identity papers but went straight over to Stachorski and took him out with them. Muraszko calmly paid for two coffees and went out after them. He did not realise that one of Stachorski's friends was sitting at a nearby table, having been forwarned about the meeting.

Stachorski's friends were enraged. They soon got hold of Muraszko's private address. He lived in a house requisitioned for Germans on Rakowiecka Street. He was seen there wearing Gestapo uniform. Several other arrests were found to be connected with him. The underground judiciary did not yet exist and there were no precedents for counteraction. So three of Stachorski's subordinates from the underground army that was being formed simply visited the house on Rakowiecka Street. They did not leave Muraszko's apartment until they had made sure that he would not inform on anyone else.

Not one of these three young men survived the war. The youngest of them, Richard Kempa, told me four months later, 'It's true that we had to avenge Leon. But if that had been the only reason, I should certainly not have managed to go through with it. A filthy job. I had to keep on reminding myself of those whom Muraszko might still put away if we backed out of it.'

Leon Stachorski died two years later, tortured to death in the concentration camp at Matthausen.

§

A second traitor whom I knew well was Stanislaw Brochwicz-Kozlowski. Before the war he worked on the army paper *Poland At Arms*, and used to go along as a correspondent when the Foreign Minister, Joseph Beck, went on overseas tours. This included visits to Germany. Just before the war this man was unmasked as a German spy and imprisoned in Warsaw. After war broke out he was evacuated to Brest-Litovsk, where he was tried and condemned to death; but before the sentence was carried out he was released by the Germans when they captured the fortress.

In 1940 the German propaganda bureau in the General Government published a brochure in Polish called *Heroes or Traitors?* which they circulated widely and in large quantities. The author maintained that the 'traitors' were those Poles who had rejected Hitler's demands, made it impossible for him to assure them a happy future in the new National Socialist Europe and compelled him to make war on Poland. The real Polish patriots and heroes were those who, while the 'traitors' were stupefying the Polish people, tried to aid Hitler in his plans for the conquest of Europe. This brochure defamed everything that was dear and precious to the Poles. Its author was Stanislaw Brochwicz. We all agreed that he could not be allowed to get away with it. There were no moral doubts—here it was a matter of carrying out a legal sentence passed about a year ago on behalf of the Polish Republic.

Brochwicz lived in Cracow, in the Wawel Castle which was the headquarters of Governor Frank. He could not be reached there, and he never showed himself outside the walls. Finally, after a watch had been kept on the house of Brochwicz's mother on the banks of the Vistula in Warsaw, it was learned that he visited her there once a month. The way from the Central Station to this house led across the Poniatowski Bridge, then down some steps from the viaduct to Solec Street. At the bottom of these steps a German sentry was always stationed to guard the army cars parked under the viaduct.

One day an elegantly dressed, fair-haired man got out of the 'For Germans Only' section of the tram and walked towards the steps. When he turned into the last straight descent another man passed the guard, who was watching him from below, and began to climb the steps. This man was obviously disturbed about something, for although the steps were wide he bumped into the first man, said 'Sorry' in a loud voice and after politely raising his hat continued quickly on his way. But the first man took only a few more steps before he staggered, lost his balance and fell head-long down at the feet of the guard. He did not get up or move. The guard bent down to assist him. The man on the ground was dead, but there were no traces of blood. Later a doctor was called and he found embedded in the dead man's heart a steel blade, very thin and flexible and strong enough. The police also found on his body, as well as money and a revolver, credentials issued by the Propaganda Bureau of the General Government in the name of Stanislaw von Brauchitsch.

Such were mercenaries of Germany who, even before the outbreak of war, collected their thirty pieces of silver from the German Ambassador for propagating racialism and anti-Semitism in Poland. From among them, during the German occupation, arose the only political organisation to profess itself 'Polish', the N.O.R. (National Radical Organisation). This was given luxurious offices on Ujazdowskie Avenue, and its patron was Professor Cybichowski, the only man with a well-known name in the group. It embarked on a propaganda campaign, presumptuously launched 'in the name of the Polish nation', publishing anti-Semitic and anti-British leaflets and posters whose disgusting vulgarity was equal to that of *Die Stürmer*. But this open collaboration did not meet with any success. The Polish people as a whole rejected it with disgust and the Germans stopped subsidising the organisation.

After that the Polish Nazis looked for other kinds of activity. They reinforced the ranks of the National Armed Forces; in principle this was a secret military organisation set up to fight the occupying power, but in practice it split the united front of the resistance movement, sabotaging the methods accepted by the Polish Underground and preparing to introduce into Poland a single-party system on National Socialist lines.

When I was leading a platoon of the Freedom organisation to carry out a hold-up of the Germany money convoy in the Skar-zysko-Starachowice area, I ran across a partisan unit of the N.S.Z. led by Lieutenant 'Grot'. Shortly after this encounter it transpired that Grot was operating a peculiar sort of concession granted to him by the Gestapo. He caught Jews who were hiding in the forests, kept the Germans informed about the movements of Home Army partisan units and operated an entirely fictitious fight with the German occupying power. Sometimes he would send his men to 'liquidate' a German whom the Gestapo found a nuisance and passed over to him to kill. Grot did not break off this mutually advantageous co-operation with the Germans even after he entered the formations of the Home Army. He was sentenced by our court-martial in the field and shot.

Unfortunately there were other Polish 'partisans' who collaborated with the Germans. Their achievements included the murder of Jews in the Polish forests, killed in accordance with the vile procedure called, in a parody of legal language, 'searching for evidence'. After death these bodies were stripped, robbed of money and valuables, dragged into the undergrowth and left without burial. It was such people who secretly assassinated peasant party and working-class resistance organisers in the back streets of villages and small towns. It was they who, under cover, in the commune of Czestocice shot at our comrades who were hiding there from the Germans. In Cmielow they informed on a dozen or more Polish Social Democrats to the Gestapo. Near Opatow they stabbed a Jewish doctor who was doing a hard and responsible job in a partisan unit of the Home Army.

Such people were in the minority in the Polish nation, and the burden of responsibility for them cannot be laid either on the people as a whole, or on the Home Army to which I too belonged. But behind them was the whole power of the armed forces and police of the Third Reich, which in its pitiless attempts to destroy us became the patron of lawlessness, arousing the worst instincts, and breeding human beasts. Some criminals crept into the underground movement and disgraced our good name. So we were compelled to fight on two fronts.

Meanwhile Nazi terrorism was becoming worse month by month, day by day. Millions of Poles had already been deported from the Western territories of Poland. In the Jewish districts, encircled by high walls and barbed wire entanglements, people were dying of hunger in the streets. In the 'Aryan' districts people were being dragged out of their homes, caught in street round-ups, sent to concentration camps, imprisoned, executed. There were more and more victims. Every now and then one of one's closest comrades would disappear, one of the printers who printed the underground press—the freest press ever known in the world—one of the men or women who distributed the paper, or one of those who fought against terrorism with gunfire. But the words of an old Polish revolutionary song were coming true:

> When the enemy makes gaps in the ranks and
> takes away our best,
> History beats the drum and it recruits their
> successors from the rest.

At first the streams of resistance were tiny and weak, like the Freedom group, but they soon flowed into common channels and merged into the rising river of Fighting Poland. On the walls of demolished houses one saw more and more often the names of gaols and torture-camps—the Wawer, Palmiry, Oswiecim (Auschwitz). Invisible hands wrote on German military vehicles and over the heads of military police guards: 'Freedom'—*Freiheit*. Throughout Poland resounded loud echoes of the revolver shots that brought down those who had betrayed and persecuted us. The underground struggle enmeshed us all in a many-stranded web of everyday duties and drudgery which gave unique meaning to life.

Nobody could resist this current. There was no place for neutrals. Everyone had to be either 'for' or 'against'. The only neutrals were Communist Party members, loyally respecting Stalin's pact with Hitler. So those left-wingers who had until recently been sympathetic to communism but whose consciences could not accept this collaboration joined 'Freedom' and other secret Socialist groups and organisations which, united under the name of WRN (Freedom, Equality, Independence) were carrying on the fighting traditions of the Polish Socialist Party, now almost half a century old.

One of these newcomers was Leon Schiller, a distinguished theatrical figure and producer. He accepted the Freedom Manifesto with no serious reservations; and he also agreed with the political assessment of Stalin that it contained:

> In this war the U.S.S.R. is actively collaborating with Nazi Germany, although up to the last moment it was calling for an anti-Fascist and anti-Nazi struggle. The invasion of Polish territory by Soviet troops by arrangement with Germany at the time of our most desperate struggles against the Nazi onslaught finally ended any possibilities of resisting the Germans. In her foreign policy the Soviet Union is using Nazi methods of pressure and aggression against weaker powers, internally she is using terrorism against the socialist movement. In this way the Soviet Union has wrecked the

hopes placed by the masses in her policy, seeing her as a natural ally in the fight against Facism and Nazism.

Nevertheless Schiller probably did not cease to believe in some non-existent communism that would be better than Russian communism. He was a declared materialist and a hundred-per-cent Marxist, but was separated from communism by the deep humanism and idealism of a heart that reacted to every wrong and injustice, and was full of human feeling. He considered himself a realist and expressed doubt, not about the assessments and recommendations of the Freedom Manifesto but about its spirit of romanticism, its belief in the perfection of the world that would emerge out of the war. But he himself lived in a world of dreams. In 1941 in the new year there was a small gathering of friends in the house of the poet Stanislaw Richard Dobrowolski, who had written some of the most popular songs of underground Poland. He had just read us some extracts from a play he had written which Schiller was to put on immediately after the liberation of Warsaw. Choruses of workers, of peasants, of soldiers, fraternity among all the world's peoples, peace, freedom . . . Schiller told us of the plans on which he had been working with some Polish architects for the rebuilding of the Grand Theatre in Warsaw which had been burned down during the siege. The rear wall of the theatre would be built so as to open, revealing a colossal revolving stage, larger than any existing in the world at that time. The area beyond, once built up and now in ruins, would be cleared and transformed into an open-air theatre. Ten, twenty, fifty thousand spectators! On the grey paper that covered the table Schiller made sketches to illustrate his splendid dreams.

In fact we all had dreamed of rebuilding not just the Grand Theatre but the whole of Warsaw, of Poland, of Europe. We dreamed of a new life, of acres of corn growing on the battlefields, of a transformation in the social balance of races, of national energy released to work together for the good of mankind.

Reality was distant from our dreams. The galleries of the Association for the Encouragement of the Fine Arts had become the *Deutsches Kulturhaus*; the University of Warsaw were the barracks of the military police; the beautiful new building of Queen Jadwiga's School now contained the *Soldatenhaus*; the building of the Ministry of Education now housed the Gestapo, and had become the place where investigations were carried out by means of the most appalling tortures. There were no Polish schools at all—neither higher, nor secondary, nor even primary schools. Teaching went on secretly, in little groups, with the teachers facing death if they were caught. Death was the penalty for most acts: not only for hiding a Jew but for giving him a piece of bread or potato; for having an illegal periodical; for listening to the radio; for not meeting the quota of grain fixed by the occupying authorities. Hangings and shootings were more and more frequent, not only in the case of those who were guilty or suspected of these crimes but of those who had been taken as chance hostages.

Within half a year Hitler betrayed Stalin and struck against Russia. Now it was Soviet bombs that fell on Warsaw. The Nazi reign of terror grew even more intensive. On the advertisement hoardings there began to appear almost daily official lists of those who had been shot not by the sentence of some kind of court but at the orders of the chief of police. Groups of passers-by would stand in front of these notices in tense silence, seeking the names of their closest relatives and friends. With increasing frequency I too found on them the names of comrades who had pledged me their oaths.

The Germans, who had not executed me a year earlier in Danilow because I had a Communist pass issued by Ettinger, were now hanging Polish freedom fighters for being communists, allies of Soviet Russia. With my own eyes I saw from a train window the gallows set up by the railway lines, to strike terror into everyone, with decomposing bodies dangling from them.

In October 1941, I came to Stanislawow, recently taken by German forces, on the day when 12,000 'non-Aryans' were killed and buried there, in huge mass graves dug in the Jewish cemetery in the course of twelve hours. Through gaps in the cemetery fence I could see a smiling young German in uniform standing on the edge of a deep pit already half-filled with bodies. In his right hand was a pistol from which he would carelessly pump one shot into each of the condemned as they filed up to him stripped of their clothes. When it came to a mother with a baby in her arms he told her to stand so that he could kill them both with one shot. Between shots he took hungry bites at a ham roll which he held in his left hand.

On a sunny, frosty day in Kielce in 1942 I watched a long column of ragged Soviet prisoners-of-war passing by under strong guard. They were being driven like cattle along Park Street from the railway platform to the temporary camp beyond Kadzielnia marble quarry. Behind the column of those who still lived came a long string of carts heaped with the stripped bodies of those who had frozen to death on the journey. The carpenter who helped to build the barracks in the camp told me that the German in charge of construction saw to it that there should be enough space between the boards to insert his three fat fingers, saying, 'We must conserve timber'. After three months the camp was closed, when only 300 prisoners remained alive out of the 30,000 who had been driven there.

By now people were foundering under the threat of the dark clouds that were hanging over Poland; the billows of acrid smoke belched from the crematoria in the extermination camps; the pillars of fire rose to the skies from the still inhabited burning ghettoes.

§

Violence breeds violence. For the sake of one's own or others' peace of mind we should no longer hide the truth behind the lie of silence. The war which we were waging against tyranny and crime —some with the pen, others with pistols and hand grenades or with their bare hands, others again, perhaps more fortunate, with air-craft or tanks—was everywhere a cruel and brutal war.

At the end of July 1943, I met a boy in his teens while visiting a partisan unit led by a man nicknamed 'The Inspector' in a wood near Wachock in Central Poland. On a rainy and hungry evening by the camp-fire the young man sat under a spreading beech and read out some poems he had written about ordinary human happiness. He had come to the forest after the Germans had burned his whole family alive in their hollyhock-bedecked cottage. This boy had been accepted in a 'subversive' unit of the Home Army, and bore the name 'Avenger'. He was the first to jump through a window of a forester's cottage in Marcula and with his bare hands he grasped the throat of a tall armed Gestapo officer called Krueger. The two of them rolled round the large room, weltering in the blood, faeces and urine of the strangling man until finally, after some long moments the body of the Gestapo man ceased to move in the debris of the wrecked furniture. 'Avenger' had a gun and could simply have shot him. He did not shoot. He will never forget the screams of his mother as she was burned alive, nor the monstrous face of the dead man in Marcula.

To save hundreds of thousands or millions of people, to stop the

Nazi murder-machine, the greatest and technically most efficient machine of destruction in the world, we demanded that the powers of the civilised world should institute reprisals. Journalists wrote stirring articles and Polish airmen, like the British and Americans, flew over German cities, dropping bombs which buried or tore to shreds thousands of old people, women and children who we should not hold to blame for the mass-murders, at least if we reject with justified disgust the principle of cohesive responsibility. The airmen knew this just as well as the journalists, but they nevertheless dropped the bombs. It was not because they had forgotten the fifth Commandment given on Mount Sinai or that they were carrying out orders unthinkingly, but because they were compelled by harsh necessity.

In the same way in Poland, under the Nazi terror, after long months of hopeless passive resistance and desperate acts of self-defence, we began to carry out reprisals, though to a much more modest extent. In Zbydniow, the entire family of a high German official was murdered. In Warsaw Home Army soldiers killed a Gestapo man and his wife and child on the main Marshalkowska Street. In successive reprisal attacks on the fast trains between Suchedniow and Zagnansk all the passengers in the 'Germans Only' coaches were killed by machine-gun fire.

These reprisals were carried out by normal, ordinary Poles. Neither heroes nor cowards, neither angels nor criminals. They were carried out by people who had always to fight a profound internal resistance, the continuous nagging of conscience, the pain of a tortured imagination. Such people had not taken over the Nazi morality, but were compelled to such actions by the need to defend the population and Western culture, and by their abnormal and tragic fate.

I too was unable to evade this fate. The following incident may seem laughable in a time and place where killing was so cheap and common. I was afraid that when I came to the threshold dividing me from those who killed voluntarily or by compulsion I should not be able to cross it. So in order to conquer myself and my own internal resistance I took a turkey which had been smuggled in to Warsaw by a countrywoman, the aunt of one of my subordinates, as a patriotic Christmas gesture for the staff of my underground printing press, and with my own hands chopped off its head. But it was chance rather than the turkey that really made it easier for me to cross the threshold of killing.

In July 1943 I was on my way to the rallying-point of the unit which I was to lead to raid a convoy taking money to the arms factories in Starachowice. On my way to the East Station in Warsaw, with hand-grenades, maps and a uniform in my suitcase I was trapped between two German police patrols. My only chance was to make a desperate, indeed suicidal, attempt at escape. They were already firing as I jumped over a barbed wire barrier and fell down. To hold up the police I fired off every shot in my revolver at random in their direction. Somehow I managed to get away and hide. The next day the doctor who had dressed the shot wound which I received during my flight told me, to my amazement, that I had killed one of the eight policemen who were chasing me. I had crossed the difficult threshold. Later it was to become easier.

So I too became a killer. I did not only kill that German policeman who himself before his death might not have managed to cross the threshold of killing which I had crossed. Later, armed with an axe, I ambushed an *agent provocateur* called Bigosinski in Kielce. On the day before Christmas Eve 1943, I was forced to strangle a former comrade and fellow-worker in our underground printing-press, a traitor called Szymkowiak, after he was sentenced to death by an improvised underground court.

I threw a powerful hand-grenade in amongst a platoon of Vlassov's Russian renegades. Amidst the ruins of Warsaw during the Rising I felt joy as I examined the documents found on German police who had literally been trodden to death—and after missing a shot I no longer felt a sense of relief. Once when faced with German spies caught red-handed I myself gave orders to shoot, using three rounds per person (a pity to waste ammunition) and as my own 'whim' allowed their two mistresses, who had also been sentenced to death, to go free.

This was however not the nethermost hell into which tyranny, barbarism and evil can plunge a man who makes a stand against them. After the capitulation that ended the Warsaw Rising, on 5th October 1944, I had to leave about thirty seriously wounded men from my battalion in the cellar-shelters in Panska Street. They were under the care of Sister Zofia of the Order of Malta, a nurse with the highest qualifications who was greatly valued and loved by everyone. When we met again in Italy after our liberation from P.O.W. camps, the reports and notes which she had for me included the following agonising confidence from one of the wounded men. He wrote:

Sister, I have lost all my family and it was I who contributed to their death. I often feel like a criminal. The Germans were attacking us on the barricade leading to the heart of the city. We had to hold it. The tanks came at us . . . driving women and children in front of them, as the German barbarians often did. A lieutenant gave the order: Fire! A moment of hesitation and fear, our hearts were beating like hammers. 'Jozek,' a friend turned and whispered to me, 'It's your wife and child.' Yes, I could see her face, deathly pale, seeming to bid me fight to the death. 'Why don't you fire?' shouted the lieutenant. I fired and I hit my target. My wife fell at once and the baby too . . . smoke covered the rest. Yes, Sister, I killed my own wife and child. I knew that they would not suffer if I did it myself. . . . But it will follow me until the end.

I remember the incident well. It was the 10th of August 1944, on a barricade at the crossing of Grzybowska and Ciepla Streets. When one soldier hesitated before firing, the commander, Sergeant Grzes, ordered the rifle to be taken from him and himself fired the first shot. We had only two rifles between us. Our first shots were fired from a distance of only a dozen yards or so. The lieutenant who gave the order to shoot, who had to make a decision in a matter of seconds, and is still weighing it up twenty years later—was myself. And as with Jozek, it will follow me wherever I go until the end of my days.

God's commandments are easy and simple. Human laws are more complex but in them also judges find reassurance for their consciences. I suppose that they could with a clear conscience pass judgment on me as a killer, and the man who gave the order to murder an entire German family in Zbydnion and those who carried out his order as criminals. The killing of children is a crime, whether they are Polish children from the Zamosö district that was cleared for settlement by German colonists, Jewish orphans from the home of Dr Korczak, or German children from a Hitler Youth school, or Russian children even if they were those of the Katyn Forest murderers. Other people's children or one's own—it makes no difference. The killing of women is likewise a crime—as is the killing of men, whether or not they are burdened with any definite guilt. To call upon or encourage anyone to kill is a crime. One does not need to explain this to those who work underground against any tyranny, for they know all too well the price of human life and death.

Nonetheless these clear and simple statements do not unravel all the tangled moral problems which confronted us in a fight which was forced on us against our will, a fight which could not—certainly against our will—be fought only with the written and spoken word.

In the trials of Nazi war criminals the right to plead orders from a superior as a justification for murder was rightly rejected. Is there then an objective limit of duty and necessity, beyond the conscience of each individual? In the era of vast death camps and atomic bombs, what are the permissible limits of defence of oneself, one's family, one's city, county, nation, of the whole civilised world?

To shoot an obviously innocent and unarmed person from close to is indisputably an inhuman act. But what is it to drop a bomb weighing thousands of pounds on Warsaw or Dresden? Can one morally condemn the soldiers of the special diversionary units of the Home Army who killed whole trainloads of passengers on German trains in occupied Poland, while the airmen who dropped bombs on Bremen and Nuremburg are surrounded with glory?

How can one justly apportion the burden of responsibility for the cruelties of war between various nations and various individuals, between the journalists who wrote about the forthcoming war in tones of super-patriotic enthusiasm and the military? Which of these military men should be cursed to-day and which, as before the fighting began, blessed?

What is the relation between the sentence of several years' imprisonment, which would be passed on the S.S. man whom I watched in the Jewish cemetery in Stanislawow, if I had met and recognised him after the war, and the load which 'Avenger' will bear to the end of his life, a load that no human power can lift? Is an undoubted compulsion, the need to defend the lives of thousands of other human beings, a sufficient justification for giving the order to fire on women and children from that barricade in the Warsaw Rising, or for using flame-throwers against German tanks garlanded with chained and naked prisoners-of-war? Did Jozek act well in firing on his own wife and his own child? And what words could salve his conscience, and yet simultaneously convince him that if he had fired not at his own, but at a German child, he would be a criminal?

I cannot find a definitive answer to these questions in any legal code, or religion, or in any of the philosophies evolved in the whole civilised world. Nor in myself.

In the jungle of man's violence against man and of man's resistance to this violence, the best and the worst human instincts come to the forefront. And when every divine and human law is broken by a tyrannical power, each person is doomed to behave according to the dictates of his own conscience and his own standards. It is easy to mistake the signposts. It is for this reason that, down the generations, the paths of the underground people cross, intertwine and diverge so strangely.

At one of these cross-roads, my father's sister and the nameless fugitive from a Tsarist gaol met fleetingly in my grandmother's house and, knowing little about each other, they spent a couple of weeks under the same roof. Before that they had perhaps been in the same prison for ideals which they shared. At another cross-roads the same aunt, the revolutionary, met a man who at that time had the same feelings and thoughts as she, and who became the father of her son. After the Russian Revolution their ways diverged. He stayed in Russia as a supporter of the harsh cruel dictatorship of the proletariat, occupying higher and higher positions until he himself was executed on the sentence of a perjured court. She lived out the rest of her days as a teacher in a little Polish town, telling the children about Thermopylae, Joan of Arc, Knights errant, the Springtime of Nations, Garibaldi, Winkelried, Lincoln; about the Polish risings, and wandering exile soldiers; and teaching them to dream of a knight's sword.

Before the last war both Ettinger and I were equally fervent in our wish to see the gates of the Luck prison flung open. Several hundred people were on a long-term hunger-strike, the only weapon of the political prisoner. He and I were troubled at the thought of the concentration camps in Germany, in which both Social Democrats and Communists were perishing. We passed each other in the gate dividing legality from the underground and went our separate ways.

During the Nazi occupation I had provided false papers for more than one of those who are to-day high communist officials in Poland. More than one of them made the vow to me which ended with the words: 'I swear ... to remain true to the Freedom Manifesto for ever.'

Of the Manifesto's ten points, only one was partially realised after the defeat of Nazi Germany. This was the fourth, which concerned the removal of the influence of large-scale capitalists and landowners from Poland by the liquidation of large private estates by means of complete and immediate agrarian reforms and by nationalising or establishing strict national controls over the banks and the larger industrial establishments. None of the other points has been realised. The political system of present-day Poland is not based on the principles of political democracy; the people as a whole have no influence on the destiny of the state. There is no system of popular democratic representation. The new *élite* has gathered political authority and economic control into its own hands. The Government is not responsible to parliament. There is no independent judiciary. There is no freedom of the press, of assembly or of association. The demand for free and universal education for all citizens has not been carried out. Educational and religious freedom has not been assured. Poland's foreign policy is tied to that of Soviet Russia, which makes it impossible for her to seek a close co-operation and fraternal understanding with all the free peoples of the world, and in particular with the nations with which she is called upon to live in neighbourly concord. Finally, no world has emerged from the chaos of war that would preclude the hegemony of some states over others.

After the conquest of Nazi Germany, Casimir Puzak, the most distinguished Polish Social Democrat left alive, a man who had spent his whole life fighting for freedom and democracy, was kidnapped along with fifteen other leaders of the Polish resistance movement by Stalin's N.K.W.D., taken to Moscow and there illegally sentenced. He died in a communist prison in Poland, when the Premier of the Government imposed on Poland was his and my party colleague from the underground, Jozef Cyrankiewicz.

The taste of the underground—my old grandmother who, under a pseudonym, wrote elevated tales for children; my father, to his death an incorrigible old-style democrat; Ettinger, the Komsomol member from Wolynia; Leon Schiller; 'Avenger', the young partisan from the forests near Wachock; and many ministers and generals whom I knew, who amid much bowing and scraping besieged the crystal-laden tables of the Soviet Embassy in Warsaw; I, myself, a Social Democrat and an experienced underground worker and even my mother, with her repeated 'I know nothing about that and don't wish to know anything'—all of us knew that taste. And in the underground jungle we all certainly believed at one time that the day would come when no one would be hunted and persecuted, no one would kill, no one would need either a disguise, or false papers, or a hideout in a strange house.

Our underground paths became enmeshed, then diverged in different directions. In the fight against tyranny so many people forgot what the goal was. For them the true meaning of the struggle came to be a matter simply of *who* did the killing, *who* used violence against others, and its goal simply their own freedom. These people came out of the underground only to enter a jungle where the principle of 'might is right' still reigned absolutely. After many years of self-sacrificing struggle against tyranny they themselves became tyrants.

But there were others, far more numerous, immune to the temptations of gaining power at any price. The peasants and workers, and the young men and girls from the partisan units in the forests and the battalions of the Warsaw Rising did not forget the aims for which they and their fallen and murdered comrades had fought. As for me, I killed many times but now, with the fight finished or simply interrupted, I would, as in the days before I went underground, certainly not be capable of killing a man, or of signing any sort of death warrant. I am with this second and larger group on the road, a long and rugged one but straight, that leads to true freedom for all.

On that road I meet people like the Polish country folk from east of the Bug river (Piotrowski was their name and their village was Brzeziny) who, heedless of the smouldering afterglow from burned farms and the baying of Soviet patrol dogs, hid and fed me for the simple reason that 'our son may be in need somewhere as well'. And the workman from the village of Jablonna, near Sokolow on this side of the Bug, whose child was dying of hunger after the Germans had robbed him of everything, on a frosty, windswept night in winter he shared what he had with me—helpful and valuable advice. And the sick Jewish woman with six small children who in Bialystok sheltered me, a complete stranger and transient, with the most unselfish solicitude. And the German railwayman who for five years risked his life to smuggle boys who had escaped from labour camps back from the Reich to Warsaw, giving them food and clothing, seeing them to the doors of their homes, with no recompense other than their parents' tears of joy and astonishment. And all those whose guide through the no-man's-land of crime and madness was and still is the unerring signpost of the voice of conscience, 'One must help anyone who is being persecuted by those who are stronger than he, any who is defenceless and being pursued by armed men . . .' And those who, in the cruel times in which it has been their fate to live, act as if despite everything, they had learned from the cradle the words of the sixteenth-century Polish poet, Jan Kochanowski: 'Bravery cannot be enslaved, and for sweet freedom it is fitting to call upon even one's ultimate strength.'

EIRE

Ernest Blythe

Ireland's fight for freedom in 1916 and in the following years must be seen as only the final phase of a long-continued effort. During some periods the people had the nerve for little more than persistent clamour against social injustice and unfair laws. But even when the stress was on constitutional agitation and when political leaders as well as churchmen were denouncing all action involving bloodshed, most citizens believed that British power in Ireland was devoid of moral authority and ought to be summarily overthrown by force, if opportunity offered.

Modern Ireland began when the Land League broke the almost absolute power formerly exercised by the Landlord over the rural population. Tenants banded themselves together on a nation-wide scale and stood fast. They demanded the reduction of excessive rents and refused to pay at all until their demands were met. It was found impractical to evict enough of them to intimidate the others. In any case there was not much use in throwing out a bankrupt or recalcitrant tenant when no one could be got to take the holding from which he had been removed. Once the Land

League got into its stride, the procedure was that, as far as possible, anyone who took possession of land from which a neighbour had been evicted, or who otherwise offended, was strictly boycotted and had to endure fierce opprobrium as a grabber. In theory, and often in practice, no one would speak to him, no one would work for him, no shopkeeper would supply him with goods, no blacksmith would shoe his horses, no cattle dealer or butcher would buy his live stock. Amongst the first to whom such a scheme of social and economic isolation was applied was a certain Captain Boycott in County Mayo, whose surname was thus immortalised. The grabber sometimes suffered unauthorised penalties. His house might be fired at at night, and, in an odd case, he might himself be shot, or shot at, from behind a hedge as he made his way home at dusk. The haycocks in his fields or the cornstacks in his haggard might be burned; his gates might be broken or taken down and his cattle driven miles away or maimed, his wells might be fouled. Few offenders got the full treatment indicated above, but nearly all were made to realise that the grabber's lot could not be a happy one, and men willing to face it became rare. With the practical elimination of the grabber, Irish landlordism with its rack-renting system was beaten.

After the Land League had won its first great victories and land tenure in Ireland had been basically transformed, a difficult national situation was created by a political split. This followed the divorce action successfully brought by Captain O'Shea against Parnell in 1890. The fiercely abusive strife which broke out amongst Irish politicians seemed destined to postpone almost indefinitely the passage of the Home Rule to which Gladstone and the British Liberal Party were committed. Many young people were repelled by the recriminations and became eager for patriotic activity of a non-political kind. The Gaelic League, a specifically non-political and non-sectarian organisation was formed in 1893 to preserve and restore the Irish language, which during the previous hundred years had been lost over great areas and was clearly coming to be in danger of extinction. The Gaelic League grew steadily; and, after a few years, was helped to attain formidable strength by the great surge of the patriotic sentiment evoked by the centenary commemoration of the gallant but unsuccessful insurrection of the United Irishmen in 1798.

At the beginning of this century the old Fenian revolutionary organisation, the oath-bound secret Irish Republican Brotherhood commenced, after a long period of decay, to grow again and to take in recruits of a new type, above all in Dublin. These were drawn mainly from the Gaelic League from which young men were acquiring a truer conception of nationality and of patriotism than had been known to their fathers. Soon afterwards the political doctrine of Sinn Fein began to be elaborated and preached with power and skill by Arthur Griffith in *The United Irishman,* a weekly paper which owed its inception to the feeling stirred up by the preparations for the 1798 centenary.

By the middle of the first decade of the present century, there were to be found throughout Ireland many pockets of ardent political feeling which were based on a new conviction of the overwhelming importance of cultural nationality. The country was indeed undergoing a psychological · transformation. Even the Orange Order had to endure a split and a representative of the Independent Orangemen had won a Parliamentary seat in a Belfast Constituency. The Abbey Theatre and the Ulster Literary theatre were showing Ireland her own image on the stage as she had not been shown it before. Novels of a kind very unlike what had been regarded in the past as typical Irish novels were appearing. Yeats' poetry represented a powerful new wind. Hundreds of Gaelic League classes were crowded with tens of thousands of students of the Irish language. Most of them learned, at least, that nationality meant much more than a mere demand for self government. The Sinn Fein policy as Griffith expounded it had a deep, uneven effect on public opinion. With its demand that members of Parliament elected for Irish constituencies should boycott the House of Commons, meet in Dublin and claim the rights and powers of an Irish Parliament, it won a fair number of adherents and a very much larger number of sympathisers who were attracted by the ideas embodied in it but remained uncertain about how they would work out in practice. Sinn Fein like the Gaelic League was a great recruiting ground for the Irish Republican Brotherhood.

The return of the Liberals to power in Westminster in 1906, after thirteen years in opposition, renewed Irish hopes of Home Rule and almost immediately checked the growth of Sinn Fein. Many who had been willing to entertain the notion of wiping out the Irish Parliamentary Party or of withdrawing it from the House of Commons when it seemed incapable of obtaining Home Rule, began to say that it should be given another chance. The Gaelic League, however, was not injured by the change in the House of

Commons and continued to reinforce national feeling while the I.R.B., in Dublin at any rate, still grew steadily if somewhat slowly. Between 1900 and 1912 it may be said that Irish Nationalism became more wholehearted and less in line with the attitude which their long and nationally demoralising sojourn in the House of Commons had encouraged amongst Ireland's Parliamentary Representatives. Nevertheless, until 1913 it was not clear that the Parliamentary Party was losing, or might soon completely lose, the confidence of the electorate.

If things had gone smoothly with John Redmond and his colleagues and if the Home Rule Bill had been enacted after the opposition of the House of Lords had been overcome by the passage of time and the provisions of the Parliament Act, the Irish Republican Brotherhood would doubtless have begun to fade out with Sinn Fein. But the formation of the Ulster Volunteers, though it made little impact at first on Nationalist opinion generally, was destined ultimately to cause a fundamental change in the whole political situation and to hand over the initiative in the South to the I.R.B. People who at the beginning had laughed at Northern Unionists and their wooden guns began gradually to take them seriously and to want to imitate them. As it chanced, however, even before the organisation of the Ulster Volunteers began, the I.R.B. which, in the course of fifty years had become mainly a propagandist and wire-pulling body that engaged in little field activity, had, at the instance of some of its new young members, shown interesting signs of resuming its military outlook. But when the significance of what was being planned in the North was realised the new spirit grew very rapidly in the Brotherhood. Development was speeded by the fact that concurrently with the establishment of miniature rifle clubs in the North, which preceded the actual organisation of the Ulster Volunteers, rifle funds were established in I.R.B. circles in which numbers were substantial. Members each paid a shilling a month into the fund and every month a rifle was bought and handed over to the member who was lucky in the draw—smaller circles were content to purchase pistols.

In Dublin matters had not stopped at the purchase of rifles. Drilling was introduced. Bulmer Hobson, the Belfast founder of Fianna Eireann, the National Boy Scout organisation established to resist the Anglicising influence of the Baden Powell Boy Scouts, had come to live in Dublin and had become chairman of the Dublin

Centres' Board, which represented all Fenian Circles in the city. The Fianna had, of course, been drilling all along and Hobson arranged that adult members of the organisation who had joined the Brotherhood should act as drill sergeants for all the Circles. The regular drilling of members helped further to recall Fenianism to its purpose as stated to me by Sean O'Casey before he became famous as a dramatist. When he asked me, as a boy of seventeen, to join the organisation, I said that I did not believe in assassination and Sean told me that I might make my mind easy because the aim of the I.R.B. was 'to make open war on England'.

The growth and activities of the Ulster Volunteers made the I.R.B. leaders anxious to establish a Nationalist Volunteer force which would drill in the open and parade the streets. It was an article advocating the formation of 'Irish Volunteers' that appeared in the weekly organ of the Gaelic League in the autumn of 1913 which gave them the opportunity they had been awaiting, to move without showing their hand too much. Bulmer Hobson got in touch with Professor Eoin MacNeill, the writer of the article, and induced him to form a committee and call a public meeting in the largest hall in Dublin to establish the new organisation. The meeting, which was held on 25th November 1913, attracted an enormous crowd many of whom could not get into the hall. So the Irish Volunteers who were to 'defend the rights and liberties of all the people of Ireland' were established.

Unknown to McNeill, who was still a supporter of the Irish Parliamentary Party, the Provisional Committee, which he selected in consultation with those who approached him, included a solid phalanx of I.R.B. men, mixed, for the sake of appearance, with supporters of the Irish Parliamentary Party. Their strength on the Provisional Committee gave members of the secret organisation a firm grip on the Headquarters of the new movement and power to influence it throughout the country. Dublin was naturally the key position and in Dublin the I.R.B. had almost a thousand members in the Volunteers. That with the quasi-military activities on which its members had already been engaged, enabled the Brotherhood to strengthen still further its hold on the new body. At the beginning the numerous companies which were formed in the city and which occupied nearly every available hall in Dublin for drill purposes had as instructors men who had been non-commissioned officers in the British Army. It was understood, however, that when the members of companies had acquired some training and had got to know one another better, they would elect their own officers. Apart from members of the I.R.B., the young men joining the Volunteers knew nothing about drill or weapons. Consequently, the I.R.B. men who had been drilling for months appeared to be the smartest and most efficient members of their companies and of course, they praised and recommended each other. When elections came round after a few months, very many I.R.B. men were democratically chosen by their uninitiated comrades to take command. But for that circumstance it might well have been impossible for the Rising of 1916 to take place.

On 4th December 1913, nine days after the formation of the Irish Volunteers, a proclamation was issued from Dublin Castle prohibiting the importation of military arms and ammunition into Ireland. An obvious inference was to be drawn from the fact that the establishment of the Ulster Volunteers on a formal basis a year earlier had brought no reaction from the Government.

By April or May 1914 if not earlier, the enthusiasm with which volunteering was taken up throughout the country had begun to alarm the leaders of the Irish Parliamentary Party who felt that it might get out of hand. Early in July, John Redmond wrote a letter to Eoin McNeill demanding that the existing Provisional Committee should be made more representative by the addition to its existing membership of an equal number nominated by himself, and he threatened denunciation if his demand were rejected. There was serious division amongst members of the Provisional Committee as to how to treat Redmond's demand. Ultimately, after angry debate, Redmond's nominees were accepted.

On 25th July 1914 Dublin volunteers were ordered to go to Howth about eight miles from the city on their weekly route march. The Commander of the day who was not an I.R.B. man was only told on the way out, by Hobson, that he had a rendezvous with a vessel bringing in guns which would be distributed as they were brought ashore to the Volunteers present. The yacht, carrying nine hundred Mauser rifles out of a lot of fifteen hundred bought in Germany and twenty thousand rounds of ammunition, arrived promptly at the pier. The pilot was Erskine Childers who, at that time, was known to the Irish public principally as the son of a British Chancellor of the Exchequer who had acknowledged that since the Union Ireland had been over-taxed. The main business of the day was carried out smoothly amid scenes of indescribable enthusiasm and a strong body of Dublin Volunteers found themselves armed with rifles, albeit of an out-of-date pattern. The ammunition was not distributed but taken away in motor cars. The remaining six hundred guns were landed quietly at night a few days later in Co. Wicklow.

On their march back to Dublin the Volunteers were intercepted by soldiers and police; but while their front ranks stood fast most of the men got through the hedges, crossed fields and entered Dublin by a roundabout way.

The soldiers marching back through the city to their barracks were hooted and perhaps jostled by crowds who were excited and angered because, though no attempt had been made to interfere with the landing of rifles for Carson's anti-Home Rule force at Larne and Bangor in April, the police and military had made an effort to stop and disarm the Irish Volunteers who supported the claim of the majority of the Irish people for self-Government. As the crowds became more boisterous and aggressive the officer commanding the troops lost his head or lost his temper and at Bachelors Walk near the centre of Dublin, gave the order to fire. Several citizens were killed or wounded and the indignation aroused was violent not only in Dublin but throughout nationalist Ireland. Within days a new song was to be heard:

> In Dublin's streets you murdered them
> Like dogs you shot them down
> God's curse upon you England
> God strike your London town.

One effect of the incident was that the restrictions on the import of arms imposed in the previous December were removed and the importation and sale of rifles freely permitted. This was an important development, because it enabled many Volunteer companies throughout the country to purchase rifles on their own and I should think that at least two or three thousand additional guns were bought. The free sale of firearms, however, did not last long. A European war was upon us. Naturally the British Government imposed a new embargo on the importation and sale of rifles and only surreptitious purchases were possible thereafter.

On the outbreak of war John Redmond promised the support of his Party and of all those whom it represented to the British Government. The Home Rule Bill, was, however, put into cold storage. We may now acknowledge that this was unavoidable iu view of the strength, determination and armament of its Northern opponents. Immediate Partition would have been the only alternative. But the suspension of Home Rule destroyed the chance that the Irish people as a whole might enthusiastically support Britain's war effort. While members of the Irish Party appealed to young men to join the British Army and many did so, the majority, even of those who eagerly hoped for a German defeat, held back because they thought that the first act Britain should have performed for the cause of freedom was to give freedom to Ireland.

Members of the original Provisional Executive backed by the I.R.B. and with the support of nearly all the Companies which had acquired arms, proceeded to expel the Redmondite nominees from the committee and to exclude all Redmondites from the Headquarters Office. The leaders of the Irish Parliamentary Party called on their supporters to carry on under the title National Volunteers. In most places the result of the split was that the Volunteer organisation practically disappeared overnight. For example, in Derry city where there had been, it was said, fifteen hundred Irish Volunteers before the start of the war on the Continent, there were only about fifty after.

I was appointed shortly after the start of the war first as an I.R.B. organiser in the North and afterwards as an official Volunteer organiser in the South. I mention what I found, because I think that areas in which I worked were typical of Nationalist Ireland at the time. Throughout counties Antrim, Derry, Tyrone and Donegal I found no Irish Volunteers except in Belfast, Derry city and one village in Co. Tyrone. I encountered I.R.B. men, however, in various parts of the area, but they would not come into the open and I did not succeed in forming a volunteer company.

At the beginning of 1915 I was sent South as an official organiser under the direction of the Volunteer Executive and more particularly under the direction of Hobson who was its General Secretary. I was assigned the Counties of Cork, Kerry, Limerick, Clare and part of Tipperary. The split had not had quite such a disastrous effect in all parts of the South as in the North. Where a Volunteer Company had rifles it had remained alive and active. Of course, to say that a company had rifles was almost equivalent to saying that its leaders were members of the I.R.B. or at least supporters of Sinn Fein. The places in which I found active Volunteers on arrival in my Southern area were Cork City and Mitchelstown in Co. Cork; Tralee, Dingle, Ballyferriter, Cahirciveen, Listowel, Killarney and Castleisland in Kerry; Limerick City, Drumcollogher, Ballylanders, Galbally, Foynes and Killonan in Co. Limerick with an attached company in Meelick across the Clare border. In all the rest of West Munster I drew blank. This was at the beginning of 1915. I found that in most places the majority of the people were to some extent pro-British in their attitude towards the war. They believed, not only that the British would quickly win, once they got into their stride, but that the Germans by invading 'little Catholic Belgium' had put themselves in the wrong, and they were rather inclined to think that wrongs done by England to Ireland might at last be forgiven, or at least forgotten, since England had professedly had a change of heart. Everywhere, however, there were some who declared that the leopard does not change his spots and that England was still the aggressive piratical power which had oppressed their fathers and forefathers.

My time was spent mostly in the rural areas and small villages and I did not linger in the places in which there were relatively strong Volunteer Companies with guns and training. There was a constant trickle of new recruits into our ranks, an appreciable number of companies were formed or re-formed and by various methods a few weapons were obtained. In Clare, however, I found it almost impossible for a time to make any progress and in the County town of Ennis I was refused admission on political grounds to three hotels and to many lodging houses so that at one point it seemed I should not be able to stop a night in the place.

My view, which I preached everywhere, was that we must be prepared to resist to the uttermost and by every means any attempt by the British Government to conscript Irish men to fight England's battles in Flanders or elsewhere. My line of talk obviously coincided with the views of the young men whom I addressed night after night, sometimes in back-rooms, sometimes in isolated fields, sometimes in village streets, sometimes in groups of three or four, sometimes in parties numbering fifty or even a hundred.

Coming back to my area in October 1915, after serving three months in Belfast Gaol for failing to obey an order under the Defence of the Realm Act to leave Ireland, I found the situation in Co. Limerick immensely improved. Even in Clare it was appreciably better, companies being as easy to form there as they had been to form in Limerick at the beginning of the year. Thenceforward, though the majority of people still continued to be against us we felt that at last Sinn Fein was on the march and throughout the winter of 1915-16 progress continued. Prolongation of the war had an effect on public opinion. People began to think that perhaps England had lost her 'devil's luck' and would, at last, suffer defeat. The cute man's feeling was that while it might seem base to have been on Britain's side if she won, it would be desperately humiliating to have been on her side if she lost.

On 18th March 1916 I was arrested, deported to England and put into Brixton prison where I later encountered Roger Casement who had not yet been taken to the Tower, and I found an opportunity to break away from the warders in charge of me and shake hands with him. In July I was moved to Reading Jail, where a number of men who had been prominent in the Volunteers were detained. They included Sean T. O'Kelly, afterwards President of the Republic; Thomas MacCurtain, who was murdered by Black-and-Tans while Lord Mayor of Cork, and Terence McSwiney, his successor; Arthur Griffith, the founder of Sinn Fein; Joseph MacBride, brother of Major John MacBride, one of the executed leaders; Michael Brennan, later Chief of Staff of the Irish Army, and about twenty others. From my companions in Reading I heard the story of the Rising.

A general Rising had been planned for Easter Sunday 1916 by the I.R.B. and James Connolly, leader of the Labour body, the Citizen Army. A German ship, the *Aud*, which had got through the British blockade was to land 20,000 rifles and some other weapons with a supply of ammunition near Tralee. The guns were to be widely distributed. An Irish Republic was to be proclaimed and British forces instantly excluded from large areas of the country. When Professor Eoin MacNeill, Chief of Staff of the Volunteers, heard of the projected Rising about which he had not been consulted, he called off the 'manoeuvres' which were to have inaugurated it. Contact was not made with the *Aud* and she was kept loitering off the coast till a British naval vessel came up with her. Meantime, Sir Roger Casement at his own urgent request was landed in Kerry from a German U boat. He came, however, to urge the Volunteers and I.R.B. leaders, in view of the smallness of the help Germany was offering, to call off the projected Rising. Pearse, Clarke and Connolly were not to be deterred by the loss of the *Aud*, by Casement's appeal or by MacNeill's countermanding order. They were determined that Ireland should fight for independence and not be content merely to demand it or beg for it.

They resolved that the plans they had drawn up should be put into effect in Dublin and if possible elsewhere on Easter Monday.

On Easter Monday 1916, as is well known, the sixteen hundred Volunteers and Citizen Army men who participated in the Rising seized an irregular ring of strong buildings spaced around the centre of Dublin. These included the General Post Office, the College of Surgeons, Jacob's Biscuit factory, the Four Courts, Bolands Mills, the Mendicity Institution and the South Dublin Union. Only ill-luck and a lack of dash at the critical moment prevented Dublin Castle, for centuries the seat of British power in Ireland, from being seized by an insurgent detachment. The Volunteers held these positions and various outposts for a week during which time a British force five times as numerous was brought into the city and began closing in on them. The Headquarters of the Volunteers, the General Post Office in O'Connell Street, was set ablaze by shell-fire and had to be evacuated. With the rest of the street down to the river burning and retreat practically cut off, Patrick Pearse, Commandant General of the Volunteers, feeling rightly that nothing was to be gained by further loss of life, gave the order to surrender. He was somewhat reluctantly obeyed by the Commandants of the outlying areas.

In a struggle such as that which took place in Dublin it was inevitable that there should be some accidental civilian casualties and that the attacking British forces should suffer more heavily than the Volunteers. It has been estimated that in the course of the week one thousand three hundred and fifty people were killed or severely wounded. A good deal of looting took place. Shops in the centre of the city were broken into by civilian mobs and plundered. One hundred and seventy-nine buildings in the centre of Dublin were destroyed. The financial loss at the prices then current totalled two and a half million pounds and when the fighting was over almost a hundred thousand people were in want of food.

The arrangements for the Rising of 1916 were made by the Military Council appointed by the Supreme Council of the I.R.B. and were made without the knowledge of some members of the Supreme Council itself. That was natural and, I think, proper, as every addition to the number of those who knew what was being planned would have increased the danger of secrecy being broken; and, of course, a premature disclosure would have ruined the plan, which depended on surprise. Even though the smallest possible number of people in Dublin, America and Germany were let into the secret, a hint of what was coming did leak out in New York a couple of days before Easter 1916; but fortunately was not taken seriously by the British authorities.

The Rising was, in effect, confined to Dublin, as the small actions which took place in Counties Galway, Louth and Wexford, despite the gallantry shown and the patriotism behind it, had no significant effect. If the plan as originally drawn up had not been frustrated it is to be doubted whether the raw country Volunteers could at that time have acquitted themselves as well in the open as the Dublin Volunteers did in the strong buildings which they seized or at the barricades they threw up. A country-side Rising would, however, have had an immediate effect on Irish opinion which might in turn have influenced American opinion and policy and have been of fundamental importance.

The effect which the Rising would have on Irish public opinion was not immediately certain. Those who resolved upon it felt that Ireland would be for ever disgraced and that her claim for freedom could never in after times be made effective, if our people did not deliver even a token blow against the nation which had so long held her enchained at a time when that nation was imperilled. The bold stroke of occupying so many strong points in the centre of Dublin, proclaiming an independent Irish Republic and hoisting the tricolour, inspired jubilation and patriotic fervour in some people but the general public reaction was one of disapproving amazement and often of definite hostility.

After the surrender when prisoners were being deported to places of internment in Britain and were being marched through the streets to the quays insults were, in many cases, hurled at them by bystanders; though some prisoners have told me that they had the experience of marching between silent rows of spectators who seemed to feel something like pity for them. If the British authorities had merely sent the principal rebel leaders to penal servitude and let most of the others off with a few months hard labour, it is difficult to say what the effect of the Rising might have been. Instead there was a wholesale round-up of Volunteers or Volunteer supporters. The execution of the leaders settled the issue. If there had to be executions, and possibly that was the position, the only chance the British authorities had of preventing them from causing a revulsion of feeling amongst the populace would have lain in carrying out all death sentences on a single morning and publishing the names of the dead with a statement that no more would suffer the extreme penalty. As it was, the fifteen leaders were sent before the firing squad in twos and threes or singly. And each bulletin announcing fresh shooting, roused new sympathy with the insurgents. People who had thought the Rising wrong or madly unwise began to remember that those who participated in it had only done what Irish patriots had always been praised for doing. Meantime the pulling in and interning of hundreds of Volunteers and Sinn Feiners and supposed Sinn Feiners from all parts of the country only meant the full commitment of those Volunteers who had abstained from action with those who had fought. This prevented recrimination and the possibility of ill-feeling amongst Volunteers. It meant also that most of the friends and relatives of the internees became admirers of the insurgents. Every day saw more and more people in Ireland freeing themselves from the influences which had made them forget the old teaching that England's difficulty was Ireland's opportunity. Instead of wishing for the defeat of England's enemy, whoever that enemy might be, Irishmen, as long as Ireland was unfree, should do what they could to bring about England's own defeat.

Naturally every prison and internment camp became a Summer School devoted to study of the principles and practice of rebellion. However weak may have been the national views of some of the internees before their arrest they practically all, before release, became enthusiastic and informed opponents of every aspect of British policy.

A general release of internees took place in December 1916 and the one hundred and fifty-odd leaders who had been court-martialled after the Rising and sent to penal servitude—a number of them on the commutation of death sentences—were released in the middle of 1917. The clearing of the prisons gave a great fillip to Sinn Fein by permitting a large number of active and influential propagandists and organisers to go into action, and Mr. de Valera's resounding victory in County Clare immediately afterwards fore-shadowed the extinction of the old Irish Parliamentary Party.

Practically every move made by Lloyd-George's Government seemed to play into the hands of Sinn Fein. The forcible feeding of hunger strikers led to the death of Thomas Ashe and to great Volunteer parades to indicate mourning and sympathy. An in-credible German plot was alleged to have been unearthed and members of the Sinn Fein Executive and other leading men were arrested and deported to England. Large numbers of others were court-martialled on technical or artificial charges—illegal drilling, seditious speeches and the like—and sentenced to terms of imprisonment. It was allowed to be thought that enforcement of conscription in Ireland was a possibility to be reckoned with. All political parties united to oppose it and the Catholic hierarchy issued a united protest against the idea of applying conscription to Ireland. Volunteers gave special study to methods of resistance which might be employed with meagre armament, and throughout the country anti-British feeling was further strengthened.

The war came to an end with considerable numbers in gaol and with the people going over in a rush to Sinn Fein, At the General Election of 1918, Sinn Fein swept the boards, helped by a last-minute collapse of the opposing political machine. Of its practically 80 seats in the House of Commons the old Irish Party retained only one in the South and three or four in the North. Dail Eireann when it assembled in January 1919 in the Mansion House, Dublin, consisted therefore, of practically all the members elected for Nationalist Constituencies in Southern Ireland with a couple from the Six Counties. Unwisely, as I thought—a sentence of twelve months imprisonment imposed by a court-martial kept me elsewhere—it proceeded to ratify the declaration of an Irish Republic set forth by the Leaders of the Rising of 1916 in their proclamation. Actually, however, the spiritual Republic of Faith and Hope declared on Easter Monday 1916 had gone down in flames and blood; but it had transformed Ireland. In 1919, the country needed no sort of propagandist make-believe such as that in which the Dail indulged. Ireland was virtually certain of a large measure of freedom but there was ample evidence that there would be no all-Ireland Republic during the life-time of any one then living. The Dail in January 1919 should have taken a stance that gave reasonable room for manoeuvre and consequently would not lead inevitably to disillusionment and dissension.

Most people who voted for Sinn Fein in 1918 and most of those elected had no idea that the country would move swiftly into a state of war. They were influenced by Griffith's account of the political tug-of-war between Austria and Hungary in the latter half of the nineteenth century which, without war, led to the resurrection of Hungary. But Austria and Hungary had actually had their war before Deak's policy of non-co-operation was inaugurated. Ireland, apart from Dublin and to a minor extent a couple of other areas, had not fought against Britain for over a century; and there were young men everywhere who regretted the omission. They were inflammable material. It was really impossible, therefore, for political leaders who completely rejected the right of the British Government to interfere in Irish affairs or to station soldiers or police in Ireland, to steer a middle course and to induce young men to continue to resist by non-violent methods. These young men themselves wished they had been in the Easter Week Rising and before that had perhaps felt it a strain to stand aside from the European conflict.

Dail Eireann following Griffith's policy set up its Government Departments. It instructed local authorities to ignore the Local Government Board in Dublin. It established courts and proceeded to launch a National loan. Every move brought armed conflict nearer. Irrespective of what was intended, every condemnation of British policy and every denial of the right of British soldiers or officials to remain on Irish soil acted on at least some of the younger generation as an incitement to shoot.

Some months after the establishment of Dail Eireann a decree was issued by it ostracising members of the Royal Irish Constabulary and we soon had the spectacle of policemen resigning in considerable numbers. A new patriotic feeling actuated most of them, but some may have regarded as a portent the fact that on the day on which the Dail first met two armed members of the R.I.C. who were escorting a supply of gelignite to a quarry in Co. Tipperary, failed to put up their hands when ordered and were shot dead by Volunteers who had determined to seize the explosives. That incident could be said to have started guerilla warfare in Ireland, though the armed struggle developed very slowly at first. The men who had fired the fatal shots had to go on the run, they were armed and would sell their lives dearly rather than suffer themselves to be captured and sent to the gallows. Because of the developments of the preceding year or two the people in general were with them in a way in which they had not been with the insurgents of 1916. A situation had been created in which the area of combat would inevitably widen.

The British authorities proceeded to arrest active Sinn Feiners and to court-martial them on any sort of technical charge which it could bring against them. More police were killed. For example, at Knocklong in Co. Limerick a prisoner who was being taken to gaol was rescued by men who boarded the train and freed him, having shot the police who were guarding him. That meant more men on the run and more determination on the part of the Government to hunt them down. As fighting spread, the population, which had always been inclined to have a warm feeling for fugitives from British Justice, became more eager to give food and shelter to men on the run.

The Peace Conference in Paris showed no inclination to do anything for Ireland and the British Government declared Dail Eireann an illegal organisation and thus compelled it to meet in secret. Its Ministers and departments had thenceforward to work underground. Tension naturally increased. The British authorities put a considerable number of intelligence agents to work in Dublin. Certain policemen who did not resign—particularly members of the detective division of the D.M.P.—felt more and more strongly that Ireland had right on her side when she claimed the national freedom which was being given to other European nations. Without becoming suspect to the British authorities these policemen offered their services to Michael Collins, thus giving him a source of information inside the British intelligence machine. As a result, early on a Sunday morning in various parts of Dublin some eleven British intelligence agents were killed in their lodgings, some in their beds. The British forces that evening fired without provocation on a crowd at a football match and several were killed and wounded and new bitterness was created.

The numerous small police barracks throughout the provinces which were held as a rule by five or six men armed with carbines, were made untenable by the Volunteers. On a suitable night an attack would be mounted on one of them by a force consisting of a few riflemen and a larger body of ill-armed or unarmed Volunteers. Telephone and telegraph wires would be cut and effective road blocks set up in all directions so that no military or police force could drive speedily to the relief of the barracks. The garrison would be pinned behind their sandbags or steel shutters by rifle fire while a volunteer crept up to a blank wall and fixed a charge of gelignite or flung a petrol bomb on a roof. In numerous cases the defending constables were obliged to surrender and give up their carbines which armed a few more Volunteers.

There was another plan by which apparently peaceful men with pistols hidden in their pockets gained access to a barracks and forced those on guard to surrender. For every small isolated barracks taken or even attacked, the authorities evacuated several and concentrated the police at some central point. Thus large areas were left completely to the Volunteers except when convoys of soldiers or armed police were passing through. Such convoys could be ambushed and sometimes heavy casualties were inflicted.

Under the strain of this sort of harassment and of shots and bomb-throwing in city streets certain elements in the police began to resort to outrage and murder while others became more and more inclined to resign, partly out of national feeling and partly from disgust at the spirit which was developing in the force. Thomas MacCurtain, Lord Mayor of Cork, was murdered by masked policemen in his home and in the presence of his family. Terence MacSwiney told me just before his own arrest that he had irrefutable evidence that District Inspector Swanzy was as guilty of MacCurtain's murder as if he had pulled the trigger himself. The fact that Swanzy was speedily transferred to Co. Antrim was, I thought, an indication that the Government shared MacSwiney's view of his activities. Unfortunately, there was excessive haste to pay Swanzy out and he was shot soon afterwards by Volunteers in the open street in Lisburn, an act which loosed off the worst anti-Catholic pogrom that had yet taken place in the North and which caused many Catholic houses to be burned by Orange mobs.

To meet the situation created by growing volunteer activity and by police resignations the British authorities put their trust in specially selected armed police with, of course, military backing. They recruited large numbers of British ex-service men to fill the depleted ranks of the Royal Irish Constabulary. I do not think there was the slightest basis for the widely held Irish belief that they scoured the prisons of England to get ex-Service men of the most suitable type for a dirty job. I am sure, indeed, that any criminals who may have got into the ranks were recruited accidentally. However, many of the men from Great Britain who at that juncture became members of the Royal Irish Constabulary had no qualifications for police service in Ireland except that they were accustomed to the use of firearms and inured to violence. They tended to behave as men recruited in such a way at such a time might be expected to behave when carrying out multitudinous searches and arrests. They were dressed partly in the very dark green uniform of the R.I.C. and partly in army khaki and were, therefore, known as the Black-and-Tans. The sabotage and violence practised by some of them gave the whole body an unsavoury reputation.

The other force specially recruited to combat the Irish Volunteers was also incorporated into the R.I.C. The men who were appointed as Auxiliary Cadets in the R.I.C. had been officers in the British army in the Great War. Popularly they were lumped with Black-and-Tans and shared the obloquy which fell on the latter. They were generally and, I think, rightly regarded as more ruthless and more dangerous than the ordinary Black-and-Tans and more inclined for cold-blooded, calculated outrage. A great deal of wanton damage was done by the Crown forces, like the burning of the centre of the city of Cork, the burning of the village of Balbriggan, and the destruction of co-operative creameries all over the country.

Murders continued to occur. There was a notorious case in which three volunteers were done to death actually within the precincts of Dublin Castle. Naturally extreme violence on one side led to corresponding deeds on the other. Because a Volunteer captured by the Crown forces soon after any incident in which they had suffered casualties ran some risk of being wantonly killed —even if he made no resistance or attempt to escape—it followed that the Volunteers felt that they had to take the most stringent measures against local spies who had given or tried to give information to the British forces. This led to some errors and occasionally the death of men who had not in fact tried to help the police or military.

I knew of one curious case in which a man who had attained to some prominence in Sinn Fein began, in spite of obstacles, to carry on an intrigue with the wife of a R.I.C. sergeant. He was seen sneaking into the sergeant's house from an unfrequented lane when the curtain in a back window had been arranged as a signal. His protestations of political innocence were not believed and did not save him from speedy execution.

The closing of smaller rural constabulary barracks greatly facilitated the flying columns of Volunteers soon to be found in all areas as it gave them not only a greater choice of routes but also emboldened local sympathisers and helpers. These columns had been spontaneously formed by men who had had to be on the run because they had taken part in some piece of active service or because they were aware that for some other reason the police were out to arrest them.

The size of a flying column was regulated, on one hand, by the need for a certain measure of fire-power, and, on the other, by the need to minimise commissariat difficulties. Each column required enough riflemen to enable it to command an ambush site effectively from different directions and perhaps to detach an outpost to block an escape route or cover a line of retreat. At the same time, numbers had to be limited so that all could be kept together and provided with food and sleeping accommodation in a single farm-house with its outhouses, or in a couple of adjoining farm houses.

A typical column might consist of sixteen to twenty or perhaps even twenty-four riflemen, who were so to say, constantly with the colours and of a great number of local Volunteers ordinarily living at home who were available for any service in the parish in which the column happened to be operating at a particular date. These local men did sentry duty at night, dug road trenches, built barricades, felled trees to halt the progress of military lorries, dynamited bridges, carried messages, gave signals from distant hill-tops, and so on. Their help was absolutely essential if an attempt was being made on a bigger police barracks because time was essential to allow such an operation to get under way and that necessitated the creation of many formidable road obstacles in all directions.

Throughout 1919 and 1920 and till June 1921 the struggle went on with increasing ferocity. It may be recorded that the Volunteers rejected the proposals of extremists that they should go all out against the British people as well as against the British forces. They rejected proposals for complete ruthlessness even in Ireland. In November 1919 when the first anniversary of the Armistice of 1918 was to be celebrated with a great military parade in Dublin certain volunteer officers devised a plan to shoot the Lord Lieutenant as he stood at the saluting base in College Green and to have the parade fired on simultaneously at five or six points on the route of its march. Arthur Griffith who was acting President, Mr. de Valera being then in America, conferred with Cathal Brugha, the Minister for Defence, who called off the proposed operation on the grounds that it would not be in the national interest and would have the wrong kind of effect on public opinion in England.

Later on when Black-and-Tan activities had become thoroughly infuriating a plan to retaliate on Britain by counter-sabotage such as the destruction of railways and docks was strenuously opposed by Michael Collins, amongst others. The notion of smuggling an agent with a machine gun into the House of Commons to spray the Government front bench with bullets when it should be crowded with Ministers, was vetoed, not because it was probably quite impracticable, but because it was realised that such a deed would be more likely to generate implacable hatred of Ireland than a desire to buy off her gunmen. However, support for sabotage and even assassination to be carried out in Britain continued to manifest itself in some quarters, and if the struggle had been further prolonged a good deal of ferocious activity in Britain might have developed.

The more general opinion amongst Volunteers was, however, that the only practical course was to continue the resistance in Ireland in the hope that international opinion and particularly American pressure would force the British Government to withdraw its forces and leave us to govern ourselves.

The truce came somewhat suddenly and, according to a statement made years afterwards by General Smuts to Desmond Fitzgerald, followed a personal protest by King George V against the menacing fight-to-a-finish speech prepared for delivery by him at the opening of the Parliament of Northern Ireland in June 1921. Consultations, in which Smuts participated, took place and resulted in the delivery of a rather conciliatory speech from the Throne in Belfast, and the Truce of July 1921 came quickly after it. I once had an opportunity of asking Mr. Churchill whether the facts of this story were correct. Mr. Churchill would not give a definite answer but did say that an incident without constitutional precedent had occurred. I took that as indicating that in outline, if not in detail, the story I had heard corresponded with the facts.

Unfortunately the negotiations which followed the Truce were thrown awry by misconceptions and unrealism on our side, with the result that the Anglo-Irish Treaty gave rise to a Civil War, from the psychological effects of which we are only now recovering. There have been differences of opinion as to what would have occurred if the Truce had not come in July 1921. I think it most probable that within a few months Black-and-Tannery would have won, in the military sense even without newer equipment. In July there was still a period of long days and short nights immediately ahead and flying columns were in many cases being hard-pressed. Some of them were very short of ammunition—in one or two cases so short that early dispersal seemed unavoidable. Moreover, the British authorities were on the point of being successful in their search for Mr. de Valera, who was actually found and arrested—only to be speedily released because negotiations had been firmly decided upon. Furthermore, the British forces had for a little while been more hotly on the track of Michael Collins than ever before and it seemed as if he could not long escape death or capture. If the Volunteer activity had slackened for any reason in 1921, whether it was because of short nights, lack of ammunition, or capture of leaders—the police and military would have redoubled their efforts and the Volunteers, like all their predecessors in the long struggle for Irish Freedom, might well have been crushed.

The saving factor in the situation was that a Home Rule Act was on the Statute book and a Home Rule Government had already been set up in Northern Ireland and no matter how things went in the South some measure of self-Government would have to be given to it. Of course, the establishment of a local parliament and government in Dublin after the Volunteers had been smashed and their leaders executed or sent to penal servitude would have brought no friendship between the two countries and would have been accepted by Nationalist Ireland merely as an instrument with which to continue the struggle against England along new lines. Consequently, I think that if the British authorities had not shown a reasonable measure of generosity in 1921, most of us would only now in 1965 be coming to the state of mind reached by the majority (but not of course all of the stragglers) thirty years ago.

HUNGARY

Eugene Heimler

What we become in life is often affected by the lives of those who have lived before us. In my case, my father's resistance against an outdated and repressive feudal system was responsible for mould-ing much of my own attitude to life. I was born into an atmosphere of rebellion and I lived with it until my twenty-fourth year, when I left my native country for ever.

My ancestors were Hungarians who had lived and died working the rich land. My grandfather was a small farmer. The weather and the earth and his religion were the three things that mattered to him. He toiled on land which was not his own, for Jews could not own land in Hungary, nor could the peasants. It belonged to a count, a foreigner, for whom my grandfather worked throughout his life for very little reward. His fate was shared by four million peasants who produced bread for other landowners: for centuries they had been pushed around by a cruel feudal system headed by an alien King, a foreign aristocracy and the Church of Rome.

My grandfather had four sons and three daughters; but of this large family my father, who had won several scholarships, was the only one who went to University. There he decided to become a lawyer in order to defend the peasants from whom he came, remembering how they had been kicked and beaten up, particularly at Election time. The Elections were 'open' in Hungary; a man stood in front of a Committee and gave his vote, and torture followed if he voted against the Government. And yet many did so, and to their credit there was a small force of opposition.

When my father became a lawyer he could have had an easy time; by serving the system he could have made a fortune. But one cannot wipe out memories. As a young man he joined the Social Democratic Party and immediately he became an outcast: to be a socialist in those days in feudal Hungary was the worst thing a man could be. It was not tolerated in a working man; but in an educated man who came from humble stock it was unforgivable.

He was regarded as a rebel when he started to prosecute the landowners, powerful members of the establishment, on behalf of the penniless peasants. This was something new. Not many men had risen from the ranks, and practically no one had been able to stand up and speak for them. His action was followed by anonymous threatening letters and by calls from the police who tried unsuccessfully to 'persuade' him to leave off. The poor who could not pay him brought eggs and chickens in lieu of fees, and the news spread like wildfire through the countryside that here was a man who was not to be broken, and who was one of them.

Although my father was a socialist he was also a religious Jew, and he claimed that to be both was not contradictory but complementary. Ancient Jewish law, he would say, was based on Socialism: a Jew who supported the oppressor was denying his faith. When the barons and the dukes and the counts and clergymen appeared in Court accused of maltreating their farm labourers, even his own people, the Jews, turned away from him for fear of persecution. What frightened most Jews was his stand against the Roman Catholic Church. He said openly that here was the most reactionary force in the history of Hungary and of Europe: hypocrites speaking of love and practising slavery, preaching poverty and owning most of the land.

In 1918, when the Kaiser's war had been lost and the revolution had spread through the Soviet Union and Europe, my father became the head of the revolutionary council in our home town. The revolution abolished the monarchy, the barons, the landowners and capitalism as a whole. As most revolutions are, it was a bloody one and it created its own terrorists. In particular, the communist terrorist Bela Kun had risen to fame by executing hundreds of people. As he headed towards our town, fear and terror preceded him. It was then that my father showed that the Jewish motive was as strong in him as the revolutionary. While fully supporting the revolution and its aims, he was against bloodshed; as a lawyer he was against prosecution without trial, and execution without a jury. Risking unpopularity once again—and this time from his comrades—he visited Bela Kun and persuaded him to keep out of the county. In consequence, throughout the revolution in the city of Savaria no execution ever took place.

The White terrorists followed the Red, and Admiral Horthy re-established the system of monarchy, at the same time forcing his King, Charles IV, the last of the Austro-Hungarian monarchy, into exile. With his supporters he quenched the spirit of revolution and once more strengthened the position of the land-owning gentry. The country faced terror, torture and execution; anyone who had had a part in the revolt was arrested and in danger of the gallows. My father, too, was arrested by the Secret Police. But the city that he had saved from the hands of the Communist terrorists moved as one man to save his life. Prominent people, his former adversaries, whom he had saved from certain death, came forward and demanded a fair trial for him; and in court they testified that, though always a convinced socialist, he had retained his humanity and had never permitted any atrocities. He was acquitted and allowed to return home after a period in prison.

Thus the first Fascist dictatorship was established in Europe with a pseudo-parliamentary system. Anti-semitic laws were passed one after the other. The first one restricted the numbers of Jewish students at University, and came into force the year I was born, 1922. By the late twenties a number of extreme Right Wing organisations flourished up and down the country, and the scapegoats now were the trinity of Jews, peasants and socialists.

I was born into these circumstances and into these dangerous times, and the realisation of what it meant to be the son of a Socialist and a Jew came to me, quite suddenly, on a Saturday afternoon when I was six years old.

I shall never forget that moment. I can still see the shadows of the trees lengthening as the sun slowly moved towards the mountains on that late summer afternoon; I can recall the green leaves trembling under the touch of the breeze, and hear the gentle whisper of the nearby river.

I stood by the window in my grandmother's house, aware of the outside world and at the same time hearing the words of the grown-ups inside the room. These words were as yet beyond my comprehension, but I sensed the atmosphere, dark and violent; just the reverse of the world beyond the window. My uncle, who had apparently always disagreed with my father's part in the Red revolt, now said that he may have been right after all. A sign had been painted on our synagogue the night before, some kind of a twisted cross. He went on to say that Jewish men and women were being molested on the streets, and that even children, if they were Jews, were no longer safe. The mention of children sent a chill down my spine.

Then my grandmother spoke. I always listened when she said anything about her childhood, because the picture that she painted of those past years brought to life a bygone century. Usually her face became young and beautiful when she spoke of it, but this time I watched with terror as I looked at her. Her eyes were like broken windows, her face was pale and her dry flesh was deeply lined. She was speaking about a night many years ago when men had come with crosses in their hands to beat the people up; they were drunk, and they hit out with their crosses, because at a village called Tiszaeszlar the Jews had been accused of having killed a Christian girl and of using her blood for making matzas, unleavened bread for Passover. There is nothing new about the Gentiles' dislike of the Jews, my grandmother went on; our history proves that we are never left in peace for any length of time.

I had never seen my grandmother cry before. To me she had always seemed something of a saint, in her goodness and kindness to us children. Now her tears froze me into a desperate kind of frenzy. Silence fell on the room, and I realised for the first time what it means to be a Jew, and felt a measure of the impotent rage of centuries past.

Rebellion is the father of resistance. That thought, half formulated, came to me then and stayed with me for a long time. Small as I was I determined never to give in, never to go under, and I decided that one day when I grew bigger I would stand up against oppression of any kind.

In March 1938, when I was sixteen years old, the Germans invaded Austria. The arrival of National Socialist troops on our borders was the sign for the Hungarian fascists to run wild. Shops were broken into, old men and women were beaten up by young hooligans, and the sign of the Swastika appeared everywhere. My first act of resistance came at that particular time. It was clear to me that the only way to be free from terror was to defend ourselves. With some boys of my own age we therefore organised ourselves into small parties of 'storm troops', and when the young hooligans paraded on the streets we did not wait until they attacked; we attacked first. In this way for a short time there was some peace and quiet. Then one night a police sergeant caught me on the street and threatened me with a beating at the police station if I dared again to raise a hand against any Gentile. After that I was determined more than ever to get my own back, and we established a secret organisation to defend ourselves. It is painful for me to recall that a young Rabbi, now dead, having heard of our plans and secret meetings, threatened to go to the police and report us.

After the German invasion of Hungary the Nazis set up Ghettos all over the country, including my home town. A few of us then got together and decided that on the day of the deportations, which was inevitably on its way, we would set fire to the Ghetto. Once more this leaked out, and a member of the Jewish Council appealed to us not to do 'this terrible thing, because it was un-Jewish and might cost the lives of many Jews and Gentiles'. He went on to say that such a dreadful act would no doubt bring retribution by the Nazis, and that all of us, including women and children, would then be killed. Nevertheless, I would have been prepared to go through with it, had my comrades not been divided in their opinion. We dispersed without a word, and I knew that everything was now lost. I felt as though the touch of death were already on me, and I was ashamed.

§

Resistance may take many forms. The most common one is some action against the forces of tyranny. There are, however, more subtle, yet equally effective, methods of resistance. The written word remains while actions die with time, and writers and poets of bygone centuries, by raising their voices against the forces of darkness, have not only expressed the strength of the human spirit, but have also influenced thousands. In Jewish history, from very early days onwards, the Prophets spoke out fearlessly against the tyranny of kings and rulers, and thus resistance against the powers

153

of the tyrant was built into the very system of Jewish social life. Moreover, every nation since the dawn of history has created men who were unwilling to be broken—particularly those nations enslaved by others. Hungarian history includes innumerable poets whose words have expressed the spirit of revolt. One of Hungary's greatest poets, Petofi, led the nation into revolution against the Austrian tyrants in 1848, and although his physical life came to an early end, his words remained on record for generations as a source of inspiration to others against other tyrants at other times.

There are, however, others less fortunate whose words may reach people's ears but who find those ears deaf to the voice of resistance. And there are other voices whose words may never reach the mass of people and whose resistance in consequence may be a lonely one and an isolated one, thus making their agony the greater.

From the time I was twelve years old I wrote poems, a great many of which, by the time I reached late adolescence, were aimed at our persecutors; and I was fortunate that at the age of seventeen my first book of poems was published. It was entitled *Eternal Dawn*, and the date of publication coincided with the outbreak of the Second World War. The Foreword was by the well-known Hungarian poetess Varnai who, throughout her life, stood for peace and from time to time wrote powerful pacifist verses. She made the point that the generation I represented—the persecuted young Hungarians—were also pacifists. Prior to publication, in accordance with the law, copies of my book had been sent to the Attorney General's office. On September 2nd the Attorney General, Mihaly Simon, gave orders to the local police to seize the whole edition of 1,000 copies and burn them. I heard the news on the morning of September 3rd, at the same time that I heard that the Germans were bombing Warsaw. Although I knew that my book of poems was insignificant in this very grave situation in Europe, yet to me they now seemed more important than ever. So, seventeen-year-old greenhorn that I was, I decided to see the Attorney General myself. My father, who knew him professionally, said that he was a Right Wing sympathiser and that not much good could come from my endeavours, but he offered to come along with me.

When we were shown into his office, Mihaly Simon turned to my father and said, 'I am not concerned with the literary value of these

poems, my concern is with their contents. They are full of reactionary filth.' He went on to say that whilst Hungary faced the
dangers of bolshevism, he could not allow poems to be published
which spread the so-called decadent freedom of the West. He
opened my book and pointed to a poem which was entitled *The
Funeral of God*. This poem described what would happen if
Hungarian troops were to fight on the side of the Germans.

> Fire from gun and cannon
> Will burn their young bodies
> And scorch the soul of Hungary.
> Their bones will be bare on barren soil
> When life is stifled, a desert will remain.

'How can one allow people to read such rubbish?' he asked,
opening page after page to point out my 'decadence'. 'Of course to
you it matters very little that we have been fighting so-called
democracy and bolshevism. To you, it appears, Hungary is a
cemetery already.'

I do not know to this day where I found my courage, but I said
to him, 'I wrote these poems when I was a young boy. All that I
know, that is written there, was taught me by this country. It is
unlikely that my book of poems could have much effect. Yet to me,
whether you agree with what I say or not, it is of great importance
that they should not be destroyed. In our schools we are taught to
respect the written word. I beg of you not to destroy them.'

There was silence for some time and then he said, 'I will make
two conditions on which you can have your books. First, they must
not be sold in shops; they can only be sold privately, among yourselves. Second, there must be no reprinting.'

I agreed to his terms, and in spite of the war the thousand copies
were soon sold as the circumstances became known. According to
the Attorney General's instructions they were not sold publicly,
and no reviewer noticed the book. But in Western Hungary on
literary evenings some of these poems were read, and they even
reached the capital city, where one of the country's greatest actors,
Oszkar Beregi, read them to a large Jewish audience. Some of the
poems were typed and went from hand to hand. In 1943 my second
book of poems was published, but this time the censors left out half
of the material and the denuded version conveyed pain but little
of open revolt. It was then that I decided that I must make an open
protest, whatever the consequences. In my home town the Jewish

Youth Organisation had arranged a literary evening which was to be attended by several hundred people, and at which those poems which had been left out of the book would be read; and I asked a well-known journalist, Mr. Endre Sos, himself a poet, to come down to Savaria and introduce these readings. Mr. Sos is now the President of the Hungarian Jewish Community in Budapest, and I am still grateful for his courage and for his words of introduction.

Every meeting had to have the sanction of the police, but they did not ask for the programme in advance. Usually two or three police officers attended these meetings, and if they found the spirit of the meeting contrary to the interests of the country, they had the power to stop the proceedings, dissolve the meeting and arrest the organisers and participants. On that particular evening the big hall was full as Mr. Sos spoke about the two kinds of resistance: open resistance, which takes place on the barricades, at which Jews are not so good; and the passive kind. Gandhi provided a good example of passive resistance, demonstrating to the world the effective use that could be made of non-cooperation and the boycotting of goods. While Mr. Sos was talking I watched the three police officers sitting in the front row. One made some shorthand notes, then stopped and said something to the other two. I was horrified for I thought that this was the moment when they would bring the meeting to a close. I saw the senior officer shake his head. Then I went on to the stage followed by the actors, and together we read the forbidden poems. There was a hush in the big hall. In one poem entitled *David and Goliath* the subject matter was the fight of the small against the great. It was conveyed in symbolic terms, but the end of the poem clearly alluded to small Hungary about to be swallowed up by great National Socialist Germany. I looked at the police officers: again the younger one stopped taking notes, again the older one gave orders to carry on. I could not understand it. The meeting ended, the audience dispersed, and nothing more happened. Mr. Sos went back next day to Budapest. Nobody threatened or molested him, and I never heard anything further about the matter until after the war. Then I met the senior police officer, who told me that the very day that meeting took place they had had instructions from the Home Secretary to allow more freedom at such meetings, because Italy was about to capitulate and Hungarian politicians did not know which way to turn. The fact that such revolutionary poems could be read that night was not due to the magnanimity of the Hungarian police, but rather to the Allied victories.

§

I have already said that I was unable to carry out my proposals for active resistance when the Ghetto was set up. What followed subsequently was a series of nightmares described elsewhere.* There was, however, one moment when as a poet I was once more able to communicate resistance, this time to my fellow prisoners. It happened in the concentration camp of Buchenwald in the summer of 1944. We were gathered together in the 'cinema' of Buchenwald, a large hall with a platform where occasionally in the evenings they showed films to the prisoners, but which was mainly used for 'selection' purposes. It was in this cinema that those remaining Hungarian Jews who so far had escaped the gas chambers of Auschwitz were gathered together before being sent on to the notorious camp of Troglitz. Sitting on the benches that night in that vast hall were almost 2,000 people. We were waiting for the dawn when we would be taken away, knowing in our hearts that not many would return—in fact, only a score did so. As usual we were surrounded by a few S.S. men who sat by the doors with machine guns in their hands. Some prisoners fell asleep; some stared into space; others talked to each other, remembering from the past the wives, children and homes which were now lost to them for ever. Then one of the S.S. men decided that he wanted a more 'cheerful' atmosphere, and ordered on to the stage a few of us outcasts with instructions to sing. It was pathetic to listen to these songs, Hungarian songs of bygone days. Then the idea struck me; why should I not get up and recite a poem of resistance? The Germans would not understand it. I went to the S.S. man who had demanded amusement and asked him in German for pencil and paper to produce something 'for entertainment'. He gave me what I asked for, and there and then, in the corner of that cinema, I wrote *The Song of Buchenwald*. Then I went up on to the platform and read it in Hungarian. A sudden uncanny silence fell as I began. Those who slept woke up, those who had strayed into nothingness now fixed their eyes on me. I suddenly felt that my 'audience' was with me. The circumstances and the atmosphere were indescribable. For a Hungarian poet to stand on a platform in one of the worst extermination camps of Germany in prison clothes

* Eugene Heimler, *Night of the Mist*, Bodley Head, 1959.

with shaven head reciting a poem in his native tongue to hundreds of his shaven fellow prisoners, still seems to me like a nightmare.

This is *The Song of Buchenwald*, freely translated into English:

There is no time to sleep, to dream,
For pain has barricaded time.
Death calls, and life is ended,
From the depth of the mountain, from the dark of the forest.
You have treasured life for thousands of years,
Incapable of taking life through laws that forbade you to kill,
You have opened the way to Satan's dominion.

Now your wives have been raped,
And your sons castrated,
Your daughters' wombs thrown into the gutter.
This is your fate and the fate of those who accept defeat.

And now, helpless, you lie imprisoned by the sky,
A sky red with flames, black with burnt flesh,
The waterspout of your blood gushing upwards.
It is now too late to live.

And yet you must remain Men
Though the beasts of the jungle do not care for humanity.
You must remain Men to die as Men
Because of your past loves and loyalties,
Because of the tradition of bygone centuries.
In your death you will live until the end of days.

The S.S. guards looked at me and at my audience. They could not make out what it was all about. There was an uncanny silence for several minutes; then everyone started to clap, and many of them cried.

When it was over an old Jew came up to me. 'Have you ever read Josephus Flavius?' he asked. I said that I had. 'Do you remember,' the old man went on, 'how Josephus describes the story of Massada?'

Suddenly images from the past assailed me with great force. I remembered lying in bed at home on a winter night, with the fire slowly dying in the stove, and my parents asleep in the next room. I was reading the story of Massada, touched by the tragic fate of those nine hundred men and women who decided almost 2,000 years ago to die instead of facing slavery. I remember the words of their leader Eliezer concerning the value of life and freedom and I saw in my mind's eye the victorious Roman army entering Massada the next day and finding only the dead, who had killed each other in a last splendid act of faith. The old man spoke again:

'And do you remember the Jews of York? They also committed suicide because they realised that there was no other way out. It happened in March 1190, when the King of England, Richard "Coeur de Lion", was about to attack Jerusalem, thousands of miles away. The Jews fled to the castle while soldiers, led by the clergy shouting "Crush the enemies of Christ", attacked the castle walls. The besieged Jews were without arms and without food, and the Rabbi, realising that to die free was preferable to slavery, encouraged the people to take their own lives. The majority of them did so.'

Silence fell between us when he had finished.

'All right,' I said. 'What are you trying to say?'

'I say that we should do the same: that we should take our own lives, before we are taken away in the morning.'

I looked into his eyes, and I shall never forget those eyes as long as I live. They shone with determination and courage and a great sadness. I thought we were all about to die—but I found it impossible to take the decision for myself, at that moment. I knew I was a coward as I turned away from him. The old man went from one to another, and I watched him as he put his plea to all the prisoners there. And one after another, they too turned away from him. When the sun arose above the mountains in the morning he lay there in the dark corner of the cinema, dead, his wrists cut with a razor. He had found the courage that was denied to us.

§

The world has asked since why the inmates did not break out in open revolt, and books have been written on the subject arguing the pros and cons. It is, however, difficult for historians to evaluate correctly the situation. One had to be there to experience the pain. There were, of course, isolated outbreaks of resistance in the camps. In Auschwitz, for example, there was a revolt of the Sonder-commando who blew up some of the gas chambers. In Buchenwald a secret organisation existed within the camp and built bridges to other camps. They were even able to build a secret radio set and to receive arms. On the day the Americans arrived in Buchenwald they, the prisoners, prevented the S.S. from blowing up the camp.

159

But the world is wrong in thinking that we on the receiving end did not resist. When we extended a helping hand to someone in need, it was a serious act of resistance; when we slowed down at work, that was resistance too. There were also men whose names are not known to the world, but who within the camps became a legend. Such a man was a Roman Catholic priest from Belgium. As I have forgotten his real name I shall call him Father Joseph.

I met him first in Buchenwald. He spoke fluent German, and told me something about the circumstances that led him to the camp. Like Pastor Niemoller, he had spoken constantly from the pulpit against the brutality of the Nazis. He had received several warnings, and was ultimately arrested.

All my life I had been suspicious of Catholics, for their record in Hungary—and, for that matter, elsewhere in Europe—had not been exactly exemplary as far as the Jews were concerned. However, this priest was truly a man of God. At first I did not know that he was a priest, but I did notice that while others naturally tried to dodge tiring tasks this man constantly sought them. He literally shared his meagre daily bread with others; so much so that prisoners used to queue up near him because they knew he would give it to them. I told him that this was very silly, and that he was endangering his life. It was then that his greatness became apparent. 'What life?' he asked. 'Why should you think that this life is so important?' We sat in front of a barrack and he told me that he was grateful to fate for allowing him to be of service. Every priest, he said, spends his whole life waiting for such an opportunity; to share food was not a sacrifice: it was a favour granted by God. 'Christians often wonder,' he went on, 'what Jesus must have felt in his hours of agony. We who are in the camps know.' He said that if he had to die he would accept death too as a gift from God.

One day during roll-call in the early hours of the morning, somebody collapsed. It was forbidden to step out of line, but Father Joseph went to the fallen man and breathed the 'kiss of life' into his mouth. The S.S. guard was furious; he kicked him and hit him with his rifle butt, but as if unaware of pain Father Joseph stayed by his fallen comrade until he was completely covered in blood.

There were others who in their acts of resistance were motivated by different reasons. At the opposite pole from Father Joseph, for instance, were communists who also displayed indescribable courage and humanity. In the camp of Berga-Elster, political prisoners, by forging a key to the S.S. supply depot, broke in night after night to steal food, which they distributed among the Russian prisoners of war. It was again not the spectacular acts of resistance that mattered most, but the small ones. But, if it were possible to describe them, these small acts added together would fill the shelves of all the libraries in the world.

In the autumn of 1944 I suffered from dysentery and was seriously ill. Jews were not easily admitted to the prison hospital, yet due to the humanity of a German Communist Kapo, I was taken in there until I fully recovered. I do not know to this day that man's name, but I do know that I can thank him for my life.

Not only the old, but also the young had their share in these acts of resistance and defiance. David was a small Polish Jewish boy, not more than fourteen years old, who, by digging a tunnel between the kitchen of the camp where he worked and the Russian camp, supplied the Russian prisoners of war with boiled potatoes. True that he could not steal from the kitchen more than a few dozen potatoes at a time, but the risk he took was enormous. One day an S.S. officer caught him in the act and beat him with his rifle until the boy passed out, apparently dead. He was in fact between life and death for two weeks, and was only kept alive by the food that we all shared with him. On the first day that David, with a now permanently broken leg, returned to the kitchen, he dug another tunnel and carried on with his 'underground work', just as before.

During these acts of resistance some were motivated by love of their fellow men, others by hate of the enemy. But, whether by love or hate, none of us who have survived would be here unless there had been others who helped us in our survival.

Such words as motives of love or hate, however, do not express the basic cause of resistance. Is this present in every man, or only in a few? Can one say that an act of resistance against the oppressor is nothing but unconscious rebellion against the father? Or are there evil forces operating in society that a man will not tolerate, quite apart from any 'Oedipus complex' he may have?

I have had the opportunity of speaking to practically hundreds of prisoners during my concentration camp days and also afterwards, and there is little doubt in my own mind that resistance operates in every man and woman, providing the outside oppression is strong enough. The extent to which it operates varies from individual to individual. Some rebel in a quietly passive way; they withdraw into themselves, and their withdrawal itself is a sign of resistance. They may not produce spectacular acts, they cannot perhaps be organised into a collective group, but they resist all the same. Many people who 'gave up the ghost' in the camp, who died for no other reason than that of not wishing to live under tyranny, expressed their resistance through their death. I met others who expressed theirs by throwing themselves against the electrified wire and committing suicide. Little thought has been given to the fact that man may not only kill the oppressor, but can kill himself too, as an expression of defiance. Others who openly rebelled or risked their lives for their beliefs, may have acted out in their resistance some earlier psychological problem. But that is never the whole story. It is, rather, that Society and social pressures trigger off acts of resistance which are then identified with personal motives.

Unfortunately, however, an abnormal society can make man helpless to the point when resistance of any kind becomes impossible. If through lack of sleep or food men are conditioned long enough to live in a twilight existence, unable to differentiate between reality and fantasy, they can develop a form of psychosis in which they are no longer aware whether what happens takes place in the inner world or the outer one. Throughout the process of life we aim to increase our consciousness and to differentiate between what is real and what is not. This we call normality. But, given circumstances in which such differentiation is not possible, we regress into an earlier phase of chaotic childhood and into insanity itself. Those who allowed themselves to be butchered were in fact made insane. This is why, compared with prisoners of war, there are far less frequent attempts to escape by concentration camp inmates; and also why in Japanese prison camps acts of resistance were less frequent than in German prison camps, where the prisoner of war was under the Geneva Convention.

I remember how, on my arrival at Auschwitz after three days and nights of journeying in an overcrowded cattle truck without food, water or air, the outer world was coloured by my inner images; how I was unable to comprehend where I was and what was happening to me. If at that moment I had been sent to the gas chambers I would not have realised the meaning of it. This is the only explanation of why women carried their babies into the gas chambers without a word of protest.

When the war was nearly at an end I escaped into Czecho-slovakia. There the Czechs had information that several S.S. men were hiding in the forest and they went off with guns to track them down. I had the opportunity then to assist in killing my persecutors, but I for one found it impossible to hunt people like mad dogs, even if they had been our executioners. Other prisoners, however, did not feel as I did; to them this was a just act of revenge. I am not sorry that I did not take part in this manhunt, because although it sounds foolish after all that had happened to us, like my father I still believed in the Law. I would hate to think that we who survived could be like *them*, because then we would be no better than *they* were.

When, after the war, I returned to my home town once more, I thought that at last I was free. But alas, it was not to be. The Allies had won, yet the forces of tyranny, working partly underground, partly in the open, were still in operation. I became a journalist in my home town and wrote many articles to enlighten my unfortunate Hungarian compatriots on the past chain of events, and as a result I received a number of letters from people who claimed that they had been ignorant of those terrible murders, but that had they known about them they would never have tolerated them. As far as Hungary is concerned I believe that there was some truth in this. Admiral Horthy, who had created the first Fascist dictatorship with its anti-semitic laws, tried at the last moment to prevent the deportation of Hungarian Jewry. In his memoirs he describes how he pleaded with the Führer not to deport Hungarian Jewry, and this is endorsed in the memoirs of Goebbels. In fact, while these negotiations were in progress in March 1944, Hitler gave orders to the German army to invade Hungary and in the general turmoil nothing could be done for the provincial Jews. But the fact that Budapest Jewry survived was solely because of the intervention of the Admiral and the Hungarian army. Horthy's fascism was his own kind of feudal brand; kick the Jew, yes! but kill him, no! It should also be recorded that the Hungarian police behaved with great courage in Budapest. They sometimes forewarned Jews and political opponents of National Socialism of forthcoming arrests, and while in many ways I am still bitter that my native land should have allowed its citizens to perish in an alien country, I am proud that there were signs of humanity left, at least in some.

As a result of my articles, however, I also received some letters that were abusive and threatening. One evening when I returned home from my editorial office I was shot at in the street, presumably by some fascists who had warned me in their letters that they

163

would do so. Neither the State nor the Political Police was able to find the culprits.

But the real surprise came when, having written an article* after the British General Election in the summer of 1945, I was accused of High Treason by the Attorney General. This was the same man, Mihaly Simon, with whom I had had the interview in connection with my book at the outbreak of war, and who, as I learned later, had been responsible for giving the order on the request of the Gestapo for the arrest of my father. The extraordinary situation in those days was that people like that still remained in their high position after the Allied victory and quite frequently carried on where they had left off. My only sin was that in my article I wrote that 'the eyes of history cannot be blinded by Socialism wrapped in national colours'. This, according to the Attorney General, constituted High Treason. I was arrested for a few hours and then released, and subsequently the Attorney General had to resign. However, many similar officials remained in their high places, forces of tyranny now camouflaged as democracy.

§

In the early Spring of 1947 I left Hungary and came to England. My reasons were manifold, but the most important was the feeling that our newly created democracy in Hungary was sitting on top of a volcano. The forces of reaction were strong, the old guard in the guise of democracy and the Cross were planning to undermine the freedom created by the Allies, and another storm cloud was gathering in the Hungarian skies: the terror of Stalinism. It was clear that sooner or later one or other form of dictatorship would rise again, and having saved my life once, I did not want to risk it again.

When I came to England I thought that my part, as far as resistance to tyranny was concerned, was over for good. I thought that in this peaceful land I should learn the value of a real democracy and that eventually my wounds would heal. What I did not realise was that, although I might be hundreds of miles away from my native land, for a long time to come events there would affect my own mind and feelings.

One cannot tear up roots, particularly if they run deep. One cannot, and perhaps should not want to, become an Englishman overnight. There are admirable qualities in every country, and one

* See details Eugene Heimler, *A Link in the Chain* (Bodley Head, 1962).

must not deny one's origins if one wants to live happily. So Hungary still played an important part in my life, while I was struggling to fit into a new culture and learn a new language.

A year after I arrived in England the witch hunt began beyond the mountains of my country. In the so-called Rajk Trial many of my friends were arrested, tortured and put to trial. Radio Budapest night after night broadcast those mock trials to the world, in which terrified men and women confessed to anything. It was an uncanny feeling to sit in front of the radio in Hampstead and hear the voices of one's own friends admit to crimes that they had never committed. Although throughout my life, both while I lived at home and later abroad, I used many bitter words against the various dictatorial systems, I always loved Hungary because of the precious memories of childhood and because of the way in which I was brought up. Now in England increasingly it became clear that my resistance was not yet finished. Things went from bad to worse; the Communist Dictatorship of Rakosi became wilder and wilder; we began to hear of arrests and tortures by the Secret Police and of deportations too. Friends stopped writing. Even my first cousin, in his last letter to me, to my greatest surprise called me a traitor for not having returned. Between myself and my friends and a few relatives a real iron curtain descended, and for many years I had hardly any news of them.

Nevertheless, however strongly I felt the rebellion in my own heart, I was impotent to do anything about what went on in Hungary. But history shows that men will not put up with terror, and the time will come when they will rise against oppressors. Strangely, my opportunity came to take part in the Hungarian rising of 1956, though not in the usual way. When it was all over I tried to help, on behalf of the British Council for the Aid of Refugees, many Hungarians in their rehabilitation into Britain. My last act of resistance against tyranny was to help those who had resisted.

While doing my work with Hungarian refugees, I became painfully aware that a great many of them were in fact Fascists, though I was delighted to find a number who had genuinely fought for freedom. Because I had been denied any part in the rising, I was very interested to hear my contemporaries speak of their experiences. I was particularly touched by the story of one man, Peter, a university student, who described vividly what happened on that lovely October day when the Revolution broke out. This man

165

suffered a great deal from depression and guilt for having escaped, and I could easily identify myself with him. With my mind's eye I was with him as he recalled the story, crossing a park in Budapest and watching thousands of young men and women marching in disciplined silence, behind the flaming colours of the National Flag.

Peter reminded me how revolutions in Hungary are always the making of writers, and how Kruschev's speech at the Twentieth Congress of the Communist Party of the Soviet Union set the writers of Hungary free. So there marched writers and students, and Peter joined the march. It was a silent procession, according to the decision of the University Union. As he went on with the story I saw the well-known streets of my childhood and youth, streets full of people staring, waving and some bewildered. Here and there flags appeared on the houses. The march went on to the statue of the poet Petofi, where his famous poem *Arise Hungarians*, written more than a hundred years ago, was recited. An old beggar played the National Anthem on his flute.

The procession went on and gathered strength as it passed each street corner, and soon thousands upon thousands of young men and women marched and the whole city was aflame with excitement. People were crying, believing that freedom had come at last. Then the huge silent crowd let out a yell: 'Russky go home! Freedom for Hungary!' Words were shouted that for years men had not even dared to whisper in silence. This was it, then; no more compromises, no more halfway solutions, now all or nothing: Freedom or Death.

I remember how, as I listened to this story, I felt that although I was in fact hundreds of miles away when these events happened, strangely within the deepest recesses of my mind I had been part of them. Peter continued: 'We marched on and on for hours, growing every moment in numbers and in spirit. We marched to the Parliament Building—half-a-million of us—to make Imre Nagy Prime Minister; we marched to Stalin's Square and dragged his huge head through the boulevards and set the inside of it on fire. Then we marched to the Radio Station. A squad of Political Police guarded the doors, and said that they would only allow a delegation to enter, so a few students were quickly elected. We wanted to let the whole country know, the whole world know, that Hungary was free, that tyranny had ended. But the Communist leadership was equally determined to keep us subjected. The delegation was kept waiting indefinitely, and our anger outside the Radio Station mounted.'

It was at this moment, Peter continued, that one of the supporters of the system Minister Gero spoke into the loudspeakers, referring to the crowd as 'fascist swine'. His only hope was now a real revolution so that the Russians would interfere.

Then Political Police started shooting. Peter heard the first shot and saw the first girl fall on the ground, her blood splattering all over the place. At the same time the Russian tanks left for the Capital, but by the time they arrived in the City the workers, armed with guns, had joined the students. Scattered units of the Hungarian army took up arms and joined the Revolution. None sided with the Russians, whose only allies remained the Political Police who were now fighting for their lives.

The battle went on for a week. Students, workers, and soldiers raised barricades and defended them against the tanks. The Russians had overwhelming odds in numbers and in arms, but their soldiers had lived too long in their garrisons in Hungary; they fought half-heartedly, and quite a number of them surrendered with a grin. Some even began to fight on the side of the Revolutionaries. At last, on 1st November, a great silence fell on the city and on the country. The Revolution had won. Imre Nagy became Prime Minister, and there were Revolutionary Councils in every factory, school and workshop. The streets were full of people freely reading the truth for the first time in many years. There was a sudden outburst of the need to speak, to shout, to write, to discuss and to argue. Even the walls of Budapest were covered with handwritten declarations and poems, many illiterate and inarticulate, and yet all in their way beautiful. There was an atmosphere of worship. The shops with their broken windows were safe, and nobody touched their contents. But after four days of freedom, the situation deteriorated. The National Socialists came out of their rat holes and paraded on lorries, swinging the swastikas. Then, on the morning of the fourth day, the city awoke to the sound of guns. Heavy Russian artillery pounded the streets, the houses and the people. The students and workers went back to the barricades, but there was an atmosphere of hopelessness. The radio repeatedly played the National Anthem and the leaders of the nation pleaded to the Free World for help, while the masses awaited the intervention of the United Nations, and searched the sky for the planes and the paratroops. Foreign radios offered help, but no help came. Nothing descended from the skies except rain.

The days and nights passed and now even the children were fighting in the streets. Schoolboys with home-made Molotov Cocktails destroyed tank after tank. Schoolboys died on the barricades for the freedom of their country while the voices of America and the B.B.C. and the other free broadcasting stations went on with their promises.

In the end it all became quiet once more. Hungary was back in her strait jacket; the United Nations murmured in New York, but did not do a thing; and Peter with a broken heart left Hungary and escaped to the West, his last memory one of Russian guns and tanks parading the streets.

This and similar stories affected me deeply. Now it was my turn to resist by using whatever experience I had, to help these people back to normality. Some of the symptoms that my compatriots showed were alarming, and the British doctors in psychiatric clinics and mental hospitals were puzzled by the great number of psychiatric breakdowns. However, they learned in time that an insane society can make its people insane.

For years I have helped these refugees and my revolt against tyranny has gone on. Now slowly, with the ticking of time, peace has come to me and to Europe, too. Perhaps in this newly found peace it will be possible to build a bridge once more; perhaps in this changed climate people of the world will find each other again, and do away for good with the need for resistance.

The world is shrinking. Radio and television bring people nearer to each other, planes cross the world in a few hours, and we are about to break out from our planet and discover the universe outside. Perhaps we shall be able to build a society without force, without aggression. If we do, then our children may live in the Kingdom of Heaven on Earth; if we do not, then we shall destroy ourselves.

For nineteen years I have lived away from my native land. I have become a British Subject and my loyalties are entirely with this country now. As age slowly creeps on the details of some memories may become distorted—but not the first ones, not those of childhood days. I remember clearly the village where my grandfather and my ancestors were born, and I remember how my father and my mother were broken by a cruel system. I shall remember these things for as long as I live.

For Product Safety Concerns and Information please contact our EU
representative GPSR@taylorandfrancis.com
Taylor & Francis Verlag GmbH, Kaufingerstraße 24, 80331 München, Germany